THE CHINESE EMIGRANT STARTING FOR AMERICA.—Page 202

WHY AND HOW.

WHY THE CHINESE EMIGRATE, AND THE MEANS THEY ADOPT FOR THE PURPOSE OF REACHING AMERICA.

WITH

SKETCHES OF TRAVEL, AMUSING INCIDENTS, SOCIAL CUSTOMS, &c.

BY

RUSSELL H. CONWELL.

商人 先生 管店

WITH ILLUSTRATIONS BY HAMMATT BILLINGS.

BOSTON:
LEE AND SHEPARD, PUBLISHERS.
NEW YORK:
LEE, SHEPARD, AND DILLINGHAM.
1871.

UNIVERSITY PRESS: WELCH, BIGELOW, & CO.,
CAMBRIDGE.

TO

MY AGED PARENTS,

whose unceasing devotion to my welfare is deserving of a greater reward than I can ever give, I would affectionately dedicate this volume.

RUSSELL.

PREFACE.

THE author's sole purpose in writing this book has been to give to his friends in a readable shape such facts and thoughts as have requited his earnest, unbiassed investigation.

THANKS.

My thanks are due to the following gentlemen for much kind assistance during my tour in China, and for many interesting facts, since obtained, for this volume: —

Hon. Frederick F. Low, United States Minister to the Court of Pekin; Colonel N. G. Goulding, United States Consul-General at Hongkong; Hon. F. M. Mayers, Her Britannic Majesty's Consul at Canton; Mr. H. O'Harra, Agent of the Tudor Ice Company, stationed at Hongkong; Mr. Henry Murray, Grand Master of the Order of F. & A. M. of China; Rev. D. C. Albeau, D. D., recently of Shanghai; Mr. J. K. Walkei, of Hankow; Mr. J. L. Torrey, Diplomatic Agent of the Government of Borneo; Mr. C. A. Saint, Editor of the *Daily China Mail;* Captain Oliver Eldridge, Agent of the Pacific Mail Steamship Co., at San Francisco; Mr. John B. Russell, of San Francisco; Captain Doan, of the Steamer "America"; Colonel Roland Worthington, of the *Boston Daily Evening Traveller;* Mr. Lemuel E. Harris, of Syracuse, N. Y.; Mr. Charles T. Evens, of the Boston Athenæum; Mr. Walter W. Colburn and the Rev. Charles M. Smith, of Somerville, Mass.

CONTENTS.

SKETCHES.

WHY.

INTRODUCTION.

WHEN the peasantry of any nation abandon their homes, and, in violation of established law, undertake a dangerous voyage across a wide ocean, knowing full well that hardships await them in the land to which they go, and confiscation of property in case of their return, there will be found some powerful reason for their action, aside from the hope of financial gain. Experience as a State Immigration Agent acting in Germany and Norway, connected with a careful investigation of the subject in other countries, has shown conclusively, to my mind, that the vast number of immigrants which we are every day welcoming to our shores is due more to their dissatisfaction with the governments and customs at home than to the advantages which our land seems to offer. Thousands of the European immigrants know but very little of the United States when they start from home, and are not able until after their arrival to understand our system of government, or to appreciate its great benefits. They have, of course, a vague idea of a land without tyranny, but in what its plan of government differs from their own they are too poorly educated to understand. They look upon any change as an improvement, and thinking that they can return, should they be displeased, they break all the old ties that bound them to their homes, and face the stormy Atlantic with scarcely a sigh of regret. Yet their social condition at home is far from being a state of slavery. Even the poorest European has rights which the sovereigns and officials are obliged to respect; and in times of peace no restrictions are placed upon his movements. He can hold property, and by patient industry, with strict economy, may be the owner of a little home. An Irish tenant, bowed under the load of injustice which curses that island, has, notwithstanding, less physical than mental suffering. It is seldom, indeed, that they leave the land to which they are so firmly attached for the mere purpose of gratifying their avaricious desires. Ireland is oppressed, and, having determined to leave the land he cannot save, the laborer seeks a home, like the old one, away from the oppressor. The United States offers him the best terms, and he comes, hardly realizing that he is indeed to be a free man. Did the nations of Europe recognize the sublime principle that "all men are created equal," our forests would wait much longer for the axe and our prairies bear many more crops of wild grass than present appearances would seem to indicate. Not but that there are some adventurers who enter this new country for the purpose of cheating, swindling, or picking up by the way a fortune of "princely proportion," — (and I am sorry to say that some are not disappointed,) — but they form a very small class compared with the honest, hard-working millions that take their homes from the public domain. The fact is that the masses are not *drawn* away by the great prize which really does await them here, but are rather *driven* away by the evils that are in store for them at home.

This is the case with the European peasantry, who, with their many privileges, feel that they are oppressed, and leave their native soil to avoid further suffering. What, then, shall be said of the Chinaman who, under severe penalties, emigrates from a land dearer to him by far than Europe is to the European, and, leaving his family behind, crosses the Pacific with no hope of citizenship when he shall have arrived at his destination? Is it oppression at home, or the mere love of gold? Let us see!

WHY.

CHAPTER I.

THE CHINESE GOVERNMENT.

The Code of Laws. — Patriarchal Government. — Competitive Literary Examination. — System of Espionage. — The Condition of the Coolie. — His Desire to leave. — Consequences of Rebellion.

THE Chinese system of government has been declared by many able writers to be "the most perfect scheme of human government ever adopted by man," and that "for three thousand years it has answered all the practical purposes of that great Empire, and is still working harmoniously, although four hundred millions of people are now brought under its sway." Without accepting this statement entire, I would add my humble testimony to that already given with regard to its magnitude and stability. Gigantic and wonderful it must be, one would think, to keep in subjection such an enormous territory! The very thought of four hundred millions swayed by a single mind, — made rich or poor, miserable or happy by the nod of a single man, — fills the mind with awe and astonishment. Spread over a country more than double the size of the United States, with the capital city away in one corner, and three fifths of the people uneducated, it is no wonder that lookers on from without should suppose any system "perfect" that could hold it together.

This respect for the system is not lessened by the discovery of a code of laws wonderfully just and practical. Any student, after reading the Chinese Code as published by Lei-Kuei two thousand years ago, with its several supplements, will be ready to declare the laws of China to be worthy of the greatest judicial minds of the age. This code certainly has the merit of being simple, concise, easily understood, and, with the exception of the penalty for treason, scrupulously just.

A Chinaman who undertook the translation of some sections of it for me remarked incidentally that it was "fit for the government of heaven"; and I felt like applauding the remark as I read, one after another, those excellent provisions for public safety, private freedom, and the general welfare of the people. It did seem to be a "perfect" system. But I could not understand why there was such a great discrepancy between the perfect state of society for which the laws provided and the deplorable condition of the people whom I saw all about me. While the Code of Laws seemed to be perfect, the execution of it seemed to be very, very imperfect.

Where the law provided for plenty, there was scarcity; and where by the code there should be entire freedom, there were tyranny and slavery. Nothing in the appearance of the people or country would suggest to an unprejudiced observer the existence of such equitable laws as are found in that code; nor would any person acquainted with Chinese society, and the disintegrating elements of which it is composed, account for the stability of the Empire by a reference to the code.

On inquiry of a mandarin whose business it was to execute the laws in his immediate locality, I received this rather evasive reply: "You Americans have a holy code which you call the Bible, and I hear that its precepts are excellent. But I never have seen an American obeying those precepts literally, and I often hear that, in the ports, they utterly disregard them. Now when you will tell me why you pay so little attention to your code, I shall be able to explain why we make so little use of ours! No doubt it is an excellent thing if we could only practise it."

The Chinese nation to-day appears, to the traveller in the Provinces, like a conquered country still under martial law. Every office, except those occupied by a few petty village officials, is filled by direct appointment from the Emperor, or, by high officials, in his name. The will of every official is law in the district over which he is appointed, notwithstanding the existence of this excellent code.

The Chinese annals give no account of the manner in which this custom originated, and, with the exception of a few traditional fables,* nothing is known of it. But the present practical workings of the government would seem to indicate that the several provinces, while living, separately, under the patriarchal system, were conquered one after another and placed under military rule. A standard writer has stated it to be his belief that the Chinese nation is the outgrowth of a single family, and that it has through all its changes and growth adhered to the "Patriarchal System." Now that expression, by such an excellent authority, has puzzled me not a little. For, upon his own testimony,† there is nothing patriarchal but in the name. The Emperor is "king of the whole world." He is the "lofty one." He renders sacred everything with which he comes in contact, and his word is divine law. "Chosen of Heaven to govern his people," is a favorite expression in

* Chinese Repository, Vol. III.

† Williams's "Middle Kingdom."

Chinese literature, and instead of blaming him as a child would a father * when he does not govern wisely, the Chinese come to a far different conclusion, viz. that he is not the chosen of Heaven at all, but rather a usurper, who ought to be removed that Heaven might appoint one who is "chosen." This has been the excuse made by the insurgents in nearly every rebellion since the Europeans became acquainted with the Empire.

It is possible that the subjugation of the Chinese by the Tartars may have made a change in the form of the Chinese government greater than has been supposed. But it is not within my province to make at present any extended inquiries in that direction. The Emperor (or rather Prince Kung, who administers governmental affairs during the minority) is at present the supreme ruler, temporal and religious. He can appoint new officers and create new gods. He can control the spirits of men in the body and out. He owns all the lands of the Empire, and all the property-holders are his tenants-at-will. The Governors of the different provinces and districts know no higher law than to do his bidding.

All the officers, chiefs, and subordinates are also *supposed* to be governed by the "Code of Laws," and to decide all legal questions accordingly. They are the judges, in this "perfect sys-

* Nevius's "China and the Chinese," page 67.

tem," and in case a criminal is dissatisfied with the decision of the subordinate he is *presumed* to have the legal right to appeal from one to the next higher, and so on even to the Emperor. But it is a rare case indeed that is successfully appealed, even one step up the feudal ladder.

I can see in the systematic, well-appointed tenant system, taken in connection with the superstition of the people, a good reason why the Empire has stood unmoved so long. As for the equitable and just laws of the code, without denying but that they, at some time, have been better executed, and that they assist somewhat in the administration of justice at present, by keeping a standard of right before the people; yet, as far as my observation extends, they seem to be in other respects a dead letter.

Omitting for a subsequent chapter some examples of the strange administration of justice which came under my own observation, permit me to quote a Chinese authority upon the administration of law in China. It was written as a memorial to the Emperor from the people of Quantung, and is given here the more readily as Dr. Williams gives place to it in his book upon the Chinese Empire.*

"First. In the department of police there is great negligence and delay in the decision of ju-

* "Chinese Empire," Vol. I. p. 396.

dicial cases. Cases of plunder are very common most of which are committed by banditti under the designation of Triad Societies, Heaven and Earth Brotherhoods, &c. These men carry off persons to extort a ransom, falsely assume the character of policemen, and in simulated revenue-cutters pass up and down the rivers plundering the boats of travellers and forcibly carrying off the women. Husbandmen are obliged to pay these robbers an indemnity, or else as soon as the crops are ripe they come and carry off the whole harvest. In the precincts of the metropolis, where their contiguity to the tribunals prevents their committing violent depredations in open day, they set fire to houses during the night, and, under the pretence of saving and defending the persons and property, carry off both of them; hence of late years calamitous fires have increased in frequency, and the bands of robbers multiplied greatly. In cases of altercation among the villagers, who can only use their local *patois*, it rests entirely with the clerks to interpret the evidence and when the magistrate is lax or pressed with business, they have the evidence pre-arranged, and join with bullies and strife-makers to subvert right and wrong, fattening themselves upon bribes extorted under the names of 'memoranda of complaints,' 'purchases of replies,' &c., and retarding indefinitely the decision of cases. They also instigate thieves to bring false accusations against the good, who are thereby ruined by legal expenses. While the officers of the government and the people are thus separated, how can it be otherwise than that appeals to the higher tribunals should be increased, and litigation and strife prevail ?

"Second. *Magistrates overrate the taxes with a view to a deduction for their own benefit,* and excise officers connive at non-payment. The revenue of Kwangtung is paid entirely in money, and the magistrates, instead of taking the commutation at a regular price of about $ 5 for each 150 lbs. of rice, have compelled the people to pay $ 9 and over because the inundation and bad harvests had raised the price of grain. In order to avoid this extortion the police go to the villagers and demand a fee, for which the police will get them off from all payment. But the Imperial coffers are not filled by this means and the people are by and by *forced* to pay up their arrearages, even to the loss of most of their possessions.

"Third. There is great mismanagement of the granaries. And instead of being any assistance to the people in time of scarcity, they are only a source of peculation for those who are charged with their oversight.

"Fourth. The condition of the army and navy is a disgrace. Illicit traffic is not prevented nor can insurrections be put down. *The only care of the officers is to obtain good appointments,* and reduce the actual number of soldiers below the register in order that they may appropriate the stores. The cruisers aim only to *get fees,* to allow the prosecution of the contraband traffic. Nor will the naval officers bestir themselves to recover the property of plundered boats, but rather become the protectors of the lawless, and partakers of their booty. Robberies are so common on the rivers that the traders from the Island of Hainan and Chau-Chau near Fuhkien prefer to come by sea. But the revenue-cutters overhaul them under pretence of searching for contraband articles and practise many extortions.

"Fifth. The increase of smuggling is so great and the evils flowing from it so multiplied, that strong measures must be taken to repress it. Traitorous *Chinese combine with depraved foreigners* to set the laws at defiance, and dispose of their opium and other commodities for the pure silver. In this manner the country is impoverished. Every evil arises. The revenues of the customs are diminished by the unnecessary number of persons employed, and by the fees they receive for connivance."

Thus it will be seen that, according to their own testimony, the practical workings of their "perfect system" was not at the time that memorial was written as perfect as might be wished. Since that time bribery and extortion have become so com- mon that they mark nearly every official action. If a poor man commits robbery in China now, and does not take something of sufficient value to di- vide with the magistrate, he will be punished to the extremity of the law. But if he is rich, or ob- tains a large sum of money, he is freed at once by the bribed magistrate, and inferentially told to go and repeat the crime. If there is any probability that the tale will reach the ears of the higher offi- cials, the magistrate will exact a higher bribe in order that he may divide with his superior. A bribe is all potent. Judging by appearances and the sad tales which come to any one who chooses to inquire into the condition of the laboring or Coolie * classes of China, there is no temple so sacred, no court so just, no official so honest, no priest so devoted, but that a bribe will make them less so. There seems to be no bonds of friendship or fam- ily ties that money cannot break; while there are no punishments so severe, no cruelty so harsh, no sorrow so deep, but that, in spite of a "perfect code," they may be inflicted with impunity upon such unlucky Coolies as have no money with which to fee the magistrate. I was told by a Chinese merchant, who has long been in business in Can-

* The word Coolie is derived from the Hindostani language, meaning simply a "laborer," or "lower class," and is used in this work in that sense only. Its common use has made it a part of our language.

ton, that when a man falls below a certain level in the financial world and afterward comes into the possession of any money he is taxed, accused, or threatened with false prosecutions, until he is again reduced to poverty or bribes the officials. Even then he will often be imprisoned, whipped, and perhaps beheaded because he has no more with which to bribe a second time. A despotism less accountable to law, or one more cruel, can hardly be conceived: and all this in the face of their boasted equity and justice! This state of affairs is growing worse and worse each year, as the tricks and deceits of foreigners are introduced. It cannot therefore be long ere a great change will appear in the "flowery kingdom."

What wonder is it, then, that the people rebel, and attempt to throw off all allegiance to the boasted "King of the Heavens," when they are abused, cheated, sold and enslaved (much oftener of late than in the years gone by) by the same power that took the place of their patriarchal fathers, and which should be their kind and considerate protector. Who could believe in the Emperor's "divine right," or wish to remain under his rule when, — as a sorrowing Chinese in California once said to Dr. D. B. Clark, — "robbers are promoted in China now, rapine and arson are winked at, pirates are applauded, Coolie traders are assisted in their kidnapping, property is confiscated without excuse, and the poor reduced by official exactions to a state of wretchedness to which exile or death are welcome alternatives!"

There is another subject intimately connected with this question of official dishonesty and the oppression of the lower classes, to which I paid considerable attention, and which shows better perhaps than the courts of justice the sad, dark way that the great Empire is treading. It is the practice of competitive literary examination. This has received encomiums from the whole civilized world, and the scholars of America hailed with delight the proposition to introduce the scheme into the United States.* By this means the pursuit of education is supposed to be encouraged, and the best scholars in the kingdom to be given the highest political places, as a reward of their merit. This is the theory, and, as the mandarin said of the code, "it would be an excellent thing if anybody practised it." At present the literary examinations in the province of Quantung (and scholars say that the same course is pursued elsewhere) are so conducted that, by a small fee to the commissioners or to the official by whom the compositions are examined, any person, of whatever attainments, can obtain a diploma. Many are said to get certificates of scholarship who have not been seen by

* "The Civil Service Bill," introduced into Congress in 1868 by Mr. Jenckes of Rhode Island.

the commissioners, and who have never written or submitted an essay of any kind. They obtain these certificates from the committee for the purpose of using them with applications for political preferment. Some are said to hold the highest degree who can do nothing more than write their names. I was told at Hong Kong that educated men of high standing had refused to permit their sons to compete for a diploma, because of the notorious dishonesty of the commissioners. As this is the surest way for influential men's sons to get promotion, there are bribes enough to make it worth the while of the government to keep up the pretence of an examination, and some few men of merit are yet examined, and pass, or fail to pass, as the case may be. There is little chance of their promotion, however, if a wealthy man's son stands by with a bribe in his hand.

I made the acquaintance of a Chinese student at Singapore who had not only prepared himself for the Chinese examination, but had also made considerable progress in English, and having addressed him a note asking if I could be present at his examination, when I returned to Canton I received the following reply: —

Sir: It would please me to have you present at the examination, but the commission who examine are to have nobody in when we present our papers.

They are more secret now, and some get through without an examination, and if I can escape paying cash, I shall not be there myself. Hoping to see you when you arrive,

I am, sir, yours truly,

CHIN SING.

It is not the author's intention to convey the idea that there is a lack of education among the higher classes. For without doubt they are as studious as any people in the world. Their literature is considered by the ablest scholars to be without a parallel among the heathen nations; and is certainly more readable than thousands of volumes published in our own favored land. Education — i. e. reading — is also general, even among the lower classes, owing to the fact that the ancestral tablets and government proclamations are always before them in print; while every fan, joss-stick, lantern, and ring, with almost every other implement or ornament is covered with inscriptions, which their curiosity leads them to study out.

The customs are such that the Coolie must read, for his own protection, but in only a few cases do the lowest classes get their knowledge at school. With the wealthy and influential there are schools with prizes and other inducements, until such time as the boy begins to feel a desire to rise into political office. Then, if the "system" was adhered to as it may have been in times past, his advancement would be commensurate with his knowledge. But so uncertain has political preferment already become that the system of educated office-holding is as useless as the code.* All the affairs with which government officials have to do seem to be less and less honestly conducted as each year comes round; while the condition of the lower classes — sad enough at the best — is growing worse with each change in the administration. The enmity existing between the Tartar rulers and the governed Chinese instead of dying out increases in intensity as foreign ideas creep in, and such laborers as have nothing but their hands to support them must emigrate or die of starvation.

The methods at present pursued by the government at Peking to remedy these evils does more to undermine its own power and encourage injustice than anything which inferior officials may do. It has adopted a system of espionage, by means of which the misdeeds of the inhabitants and officials are supposed to be reported at the capital. For a time it may seem to strengthen the power of the government by making it dreaded. But the cruel-

* Nevius's "China and the Chinese," p. 60; Doolittle's "Social Life of the Chinese," Vol. I. pp. 428, 431; Williams's "Middle Kingdom," Vol. I. p. 451.

ties and extortions to which it gives rise must sooner or later arouse a spirit of rebellion that no despotic power on earth can quell. Not only are salaried men sent out through all the towns to associate with thieves and swindlers and to report their doings, but rewards are offered to any person who shall expose a criminal act, or be instrumental in bringing the culprit to justice. Strange as it may seem, this detective system encourages crime, while it arrests, fines, and imprisons the innocent. Charges crowd the magisterial courts, made against innocent persons, with the hope of getting a reward, and as money is better evidence than human testimony, the party that bribes the mandarin will get his case. Detectives steal and rob with impunity, and lay the charge upon some poor friendless Coolie who has not the education or means to defend himself, and he suffers for the sins of the detectives, while the latter receives the reward. All these official detectives, and many other persons who make espionage their business, are fast accumulating fortunes and are building up a moneyed aristocracy, the founders of which are taken from the most unscrupulous men in the Empire. How changed the state of society since the time when the Emperor was conscientious, the officials honest, and the people practised the benevolence of Boodah and the morality of Confucius! Driving into exile their best friends, the Coolies, by their own short-sighted dishonesty! The effect of this bad policy is already apparent in the agricultural districts of China itself, and soon the officials must call back the Coolie, and give him his rights, or take his place at the plough and threshing-floor. A writer from Nanking having an extended knowledge of China, and who is the very best authority on this subject,* says, with regard to the country overrun by the late rebellion, that the present state of the country is a veritable wilderness. As far as eye can reach, the coarse annual grasses, which in China invade so rapidly neglected ground, extend sometimes for miles, and not a field can be seen under cultivation. The roads are broken up and almost obliterated, while beasts of burden are scarcely met with. Looked at from an eminence, long rows of villages are to be seen; their brown and moss-grown walls and roofs scarcely contrasting at this season of the year with the decaying grasses of last summer's crop. Yet a nearer approach discovers towns without inhabitants; their houses burnt or deserted: while a few grovelling wretches, scarcely subsisting, struggle for existence in the midst of teeming soils. In fact, we have a country here for all practical purposes just as new as the Western States in America, waiting only for the hand of man to snatch its riches. The story of its present deso-

* European Supreme Court Journal, Shanghai.

lation is a short one: bad government and consequent rebellions have proved alike destructive to innocent and guilty. A Roman Catholic missionary who has labored among these scenes since the establishment of Imperial authority speaks in sad terms of the utter demoralization of the people. Their old men and women ruthlessly slaughtered, their young men pressed into the service of the Taipings; their young women carried off and used for the vilest purposes, while their children were daily forced to see these spectacles of blood and the most revolting crimes perpetrated under their eyes; it is but natural that the few survivors should have sunk in the scale of humanity. Families, he tells us, have been utterly broken up; husbands seek for wives, wives for husbands; parents and children wander about unaware of each other's existence. Amongst his own flock he finds the utmost difficulties; marriage, elsewhere amongst the Chinese hedged in with so many forms, is held in light esteem; often has he to refuse the rites of the church, till proof of the legality of the ceremony can be adduced.

Such is the state to which a fertile and populous country has been reduced by the shortcomings of its government. When the Emperor Yaou, according to the *Shoo King*, in his old age desired to appoint a successor on whom the labor of consolidating the new empire should rest, Shun, though one of the lower orders, was chosen; his father was obstinate and unprincipled, his mother insincere, and his brother arrogant; yet amidst all these discordant elements he contrived to live in harmony, and exercised over his relations an influence for good. The moral of the tale has since been persistently misapplied by the government of China. As a paternal system it has ignored the duties it owes to its subjects; forgetting that history, in recording the elevation of Shun, has not sought to condone the unprincipled conduct of the father, but to praise the supereminent virtues of the son; who, as having had a sad experience of the effects of ill conduct in the heads of a family, could not fail to apply to the affairs of the empire the wisdom he had learned in his father's household. Let us inquire, then, the course which the Chinese government has taken to restore this country to its former condition. An opportunity has been offered, rare in the annals of the world, of founding anew an old empire: the means are at hand; the fabric of government has not been so entirely disorganized as to deprive it of the power of reform. Yet, with the single exception of exempting from the payment of the land tax for two years all new settlers who shall undertake to cultivate plots of ground within the district, nothing whatever has been done; and it seems doubtful whether, in the absence of better means of intercommunication, such a remission, unaccompanied by more decisive action on the part of Government, as encouraging the influx of pauper settlers, may not have an evil tendency.

In suggesting a practical course to the Chinese we do not fail to remember that the prosperity of each rests on the well-being of all. We have passed the day when it could be urged that foreign interests were best served by the misfortunes of China. The effects of political disturbances in China and in the Far West, as well as the monetary panic of 1866, have been experienced by both native and foreign traders alike, and in the present distressed state of trade in China we recognize the natural results of the crisis of rebellion through which the country has passed.

What is required in the devastated districts of China, as in all other new countries, is, in the first place, labor and capital to prepare and till the soil; next to these, if at all inferior, are the means of transport. *It may almost seem a paradox to affirm that labor is scarce in China, yet all experience goes to prove it:* hundreds of poor wretches wander about or nestle in the large cities, but most of these now bear the undeniable brand of confirmed mendicancy. The features so easily recognized among the followers of the Tien Wang, will seldom be looked for in vain among a crowd of Chinese beggars; the habits of rapine and cruelty fostered in the Taiping ranks were far too strong to be eradicated. But even with a superabundance of labor the settler on the deserted soil finds it impossible to bring his land under cultivation without capital. The old ties of family are broken up; he finds he must pay for his daily labor as well as for the seed to put in the ground. Unless he meet with some exterior support he rapidly falls to the condition of a squatter, and such, in fact, is the position of most of the inhabitants.

Few, if any, better roads were to be found fifty years ago in Europe than that which connected the cities of Nanking and Chinkiang; it possessed all the features of a good road; the route was the most direct possible, every care had been taken in its engineering; the levels were good, cuttings having been made where hills were intersected, and embankments in the open plains; the bridges were substantial and well designed for traffic, while the road for a width of 14 or 15 feet was carefully paved with brick. In fact a coach and four could readily have traversed the entire length, with less discomfort than would be met with on many of the mail roads in England. At present the condition of this road is a standing disgrace to the provincial authorities. Here and there indeed some fragment displays the care taken by former governments, but the greater portion has fallen into the last stage of decay: the bricks have been rooted up, the stones worn by the wheels of barrows lie in confusion; a day's rain renders the track impassable and forces passengers to prefer the waste ground at the sides, while repairs, where attempted, have been executed in such a style as renders the remedy worse than the disease. One or two stones represent many of the bridges, and in many places streams coming down from the hills form deep channels along the track. It is scarcely passable for the pack-mules in fine weather, at other seasons it is actually impracticable. When this is the state of the main road, the condition of the inferior ones may easily be guessed; in fact, at the best of weathers it is impossible for the wheeled vehicles of the country to traverse them. Without navigable canals and with impassable roads, it is manifestly impossible for the harvests, however abundant, to be brought to market. Even on the main road rice fetches 30 per cent less than at Chinkiang; in the interior no market can be said to exist. Yet all this occurs during the time of famine in the northern provinces, when the Peking government actually sends down a Commissioner to Hongkong to arrange for the import of foreign rices. No stronger proof could be urged of its helpless imbecility. With good roads intersecting the country, and good crops coming in, with a moderate population living in prosperous circumstances, how much of the *present discontent in China* might be alleviated.

CHAPTER II.

CHINESE SUPERSTITION.

Different Religions. — The strange mixture of Ideas. — The Coolies' Purgatory. — Metempsychosis. — Fear of pending National Evil. — Its effect upon Emigration. — Remarkable Letter from a Chinese Merchant in California.

AMONG that class of Chinese who emigrate to America there is in reality no established religion. They are the laboring classes of the Canton District, and have had but little time or opportunity for study or reflection upon religious subjects. In fact, the tenets of the different religions are so intermingled that the priests themselves have considerable difficulty in deciding which is Tauist and which is Boodist.

Boodism consists in the worship of a divinity, which, in connection with inferior spirits, has especial regard for good works, and rewards those who live virtuous lives with a happy or oblivious hereafter. Its devotees believe in the transmigration of souls, and in a former state of existence when the present souls of men were the spirits of beasts, birds, or reptiles. They believe also in a kind of purgatory to which all souls go after death to be prepared for their future existence as earthly beings. During their stay in purgatory these souls have need of the "necessities of life," and the friends on earth must supply them with money or they will suffer. Connected with this belief are a thousand superstitions and fables, to which reference cannot be made here.

Tauism is a kind of materialism, the devotees of which believe that the earth, the planets, and each separate thing upon them, is endowed with an intelligent soul. Connected with it is a belief in the mysterious influence of the moon and stars upon the destinies of men, and the idea that by alchemy may yet be found a way of turning iron or earth into gold or silver. There are in this, as in the Boodist religion, any number of gods, the greatest of which is worshipped under the name of Laoots, or "The Old Boy," and the most merciful of which is Lootyoo, the god of medicine.

There is another sect to which all the government officials ostensibly belong, which cannot be called a religion, but rather the absence of religion. The adherents of this doctrine claim to be followers of the Confucian teachings, and practicers of those rationalistic theories to which his precepts tend. Confucius recognized no God, but went about teaching morality, and advising people to practise it for their own welfare on earth. Perhaps I cannot do better than to quote a few extracts from Dr. Legg's translation of the Confucian analects to show the manner in which his teachings have been preserved.*

"The stable being burned down when he was at court, on his return he said, 'Has any man been hurt?' He did not ask about the horses."

"When any of his friends died, if he had no relations who could be depended upon for the necessary offices he would say, 'I will bury him.'"

"To any person in mourning he bowed forward to the cross-bar of his carriage."

"The master said, 'To go beyond is as wrong as to fall short.'"

"The master said, 'There is Hwuy. He has nearly attained to perfect virtue. He is often in want.'"

"Yen Yuen asked about perfect virtue. The master said, 'To subdue one's self and return to propriety is perfect virtue.'"

"The master said, 'In hearing litigations I am like any other body. What is necessary is to cause the people to have no litigations.'"

Beside the Boodist, Tauist, and Confucian sects, which may be said to be the heathen religions of China, there is a large number of Mahometans in the empire, and in some of the cities in the Prov-

* Life and Teachings of Confucius, pp. 185, 186.

inces of Shensi and Shansi the mosque and the Boodist temple are said to stand side by side. There is also a large number of semi-Catholics who have retained some of the doctrines preached by the Catholic missionaries in Abbé Huc's time, and combined them with those of one or the other of the heathen sects. Beside these there are quite a large number of fresh converts to the Catholic religion, a few Jews, and still fewer Protestants.

To the educated Chinaman, who, if he is a scholar at all, is usually a great one, these religions may have a distinct and separate significance. But I am sorry to say that by a careful investigation, assisted by missionaries and native scholars, I have reluctantly arrived at the conclusion that the laborers of China as a class have no clear idea of any one religion. The sadder is it, because where there is no settled belief to assail there is but little hope for the Christian missionary. The belief of this Coolie class (if their faith may be called a belief at all) is made up by a strange combination of all that is unnatural and mysterious to be found in the faith of all of the several sects. They pay equal devotion to the gods of each. Boodist, Tauist, Confucian, Mahometan, Jewish, Catholic, and Atheistic ideas, combined with a superstition that makes every circumstance in life to portend some evil or good, serves to make up the faith of the class from whence come the laborers for America. There may be something poetical about the mind that

> "Finds tongues in trees, books in the running brooks,
> Sermons in stones, and good in everything";

but the Coolies' belief that trees, brooks, and stones are endowed with real intelligence, and can injure or benefit man as they may happen to feel, is far from being a poetical one. It keeps the soul in constant alarm and loads the mind with care. When combined with the other Coolie ideas, that the heavens, the earth, the sea, the sky, paradise, and hell are filled with wrangling, fickle, avaricious gods, whose only occupation is to fight over the disposition that shall be made of man here and his soul hereafter, it becomes doubly terrible. Then the beasts, the birds, the fish, the reptiles, and the insects are supposed to contain the souls of future generations, or of the generation that is past. To really believe that his deceased grandmother is a cow, his grandfather an alligator, his little sister a codfish, his father a buffalo, and his mother in Hades wandering about in starvation alone, because he has no means to purchase and burn "mock money" to supply her necessities, is as terrible and harassing to the believer as it is ridiculous to us. His life is a state of fear. Blue devils hold dire calamities over his head at night, and white-robed imps repeat the threatenings by day. He will be punished by one god if he does an act, and scourged by another if he does it not. All his time for devotion is used in appeasing the wrath of the angry gods. Yet if he pays any respect to one and not the same to the others there will be a jealous war in the abode of the gods, the result of which will be a combined attack upon the defenceless worshipper. Merit seems to have little or nothing to do with the question, and if the devotee has nothing of his own with which to keep these gods quiet he must steal something to offer them, and after he has stolen the sacrifice he is kept in constant fear lest the gods go and tell the mandarin of the peculation and have him punished. This is the state of mind in which missionaries and other inquirers often find the Coolie believer. But as in our land there are thousands of ostensible Christians who in times of prosperity are not Christians at all, so in China, when the Benevolent gods prevail (and they are supposed to be good without sacrifices) the Coolie forgets his fears, and with a vague hope that he will live and prosper many years, and be made a lion when he dies, he goes and comes to his work in the shop or rice-field carelessly happy.

This superstitious religion of the lower classes places a great and dangerous power in the hands of the rulers. They may be never so cruel and the ignorant Coolie will exculpate them from all blame and, still thinking the Chinese government the best on earth, will attribute all his hardships to the ill-will of some devil-god whom he has offended. This has been the case for the past twelve years. The tyranny of the rulers, shown by the laxity in the execution of justice, high taxation, and low wages, combined with a threatened famine, has awakened the fears of the Coolie classes, and made them doubly vigilant in their sacrifices to the evil spirits. This feeling so strongly excited in 1853, and again in 1859, has been kept up and increased each year by the exactions of the government, until the religious condition of many at present is a state of terror.

The hardships and tyranny continuing for so long a time, superstitious stories creep into circulation to account for the calamity that seems to have befallen the laboring classes. Some said the Emperor was an impostor, and rebelled; some said that it was because they paid all their money into the national treasury, and had none left with which to pay proper respect to the gods, and, refusing to pay their taxes, were sold into slavery. Taxes grew heavier, wages less, slaves more frequent, the necessity for destroying their children more urgent; and, as they must account for it in some way, they began to believe that the whole nation had incurred the hatred of the gods, and, until certain wonderful signs were seen, there would be no relief. Those signs have not yet been seen, and while they wait, many leave for other countries, hoping that the ill-will of the gods will not follow them, and feeling that they can return when prosperity is restored, and bribe their way out of the penalties of the law against leaving the country.* Many are the superstitious tales that are told in this connection, beside which our legends of blood in the sky before the Revolution, and armies in the clouds at the beginning of the great rebellion, are Liliputian indeed. These dark omens and strange visions portending future evil to the masses have received great credence among the inhabitants in the vicinity of Canton, and I was told by European officials in Chinese employ that these superstitions were actually driving a part of the people away from their homes. Seized with an unaccountable fear of coming, evil they determine to leave the country for a season, and subsequent chapters will show to what land they go.

It is with great pleasure that I give place to a letter written by a Chinese gentleman of educa-

* In the agreement made with the Chinese government through Prince Kung, in 1866, by the English, French, and American governments, it was stipulated that "no obstacles shall be thrown in the way of Chinese emigration." But no change has ever been made in the local laws concerning it, and in all the districts it is considered as great a misdemeanor now to leave China as it was before that treaty.

tion and position who has been in Europe and the eastern part of the United States, and whose testimony upon this matter of Chinese superstition is beyond question.

SACRAMENTO, CALIFORNIA, January 27th.

DEAR SIR, — It is with some doubt that I take my pen in hand to communicate with you. Your kind note of the 15th found me full of business for my countrymen, and I must beg pardon for this long delay. I hope you don't mean to publish what I write, as I am a poor scholar in European, and would be not pleased to have you do so. If so, do not say I write it. My opinion about the religion which you call "superstition" is found in this: I think the people are poor, and as they have little chance to grow in education in China they believe what is told them. I have always believed in Confucius, and am still. The difficulty which our King (we call him *Woong tye* in China) has with this part of our people, in his governing, is because they cannot understand. They think they have bad time in China, and some Ny-koos (nuns) tells them that there will come a famine soon time and they frighten at it and say, 'How can we live? We have much family and no rice, no fish.' Then they hear that they can come to this country and get pay. So they come. They think some time business will be better and the famine gone. Then they will go back. They don't all so think, and some that have been here in Sacramento for a long time don't seem to be anything in belief, but there in China they get strange ideas that makes them uneasy and want to go away. How bad I should feel, and I think your people would if the things do happen that my people speak about. They expect to see in China all slaves and no rice at all, which would be sad. They tell me strange stories about their seeing Buddah with a great sword from horizon to horizon, and that they find blood in the clothes when they wash, and that they see China sometimes in the sky with a great smoke under it. All much fearful, and so they don't go back when ready. They ask the Shang-shang (god) and he won't say yes or no, so they think he don't want to tell. You must not think anything of it, for they are poor and not knowing. They would know better if they could. I cannot think many of them here came because they not liked China. They want money and a place where they do not frighten. They like here and so do I. But we will all go home some time when the Shang-shang (god) thinks we become happy. My countrymen are in much business and they learn much too. They are not so foolish as those who first come. I don't know what I can say about your question [*more*]. They were not wise who told you that my countrymen like not China. All of us will go back when we get little older. China suffers at this time and we weep too.

Please write me and say if you love this letter.*

* A money broker and rice merchant.

CHAPTER III.

CHINESE CHARACTER.

Various Opinions. — Pride, Fear, and Cunning. — An interesting Incident of a Coolie's Shrewdness. — Policy of the Government. — The Affections. — Imitative Powers. — What China might be. — The Coolie's Desire to be buried in China, and the Motives which create it. — Burial in the East Indian Colonies.

PERHAPS I cannot do better than to devote one chapter to the discussion of those characteristics which distinguish the Chinese from other races. It is a subject, however, upon which there may be a variety of opinions, owing to the different circumstances in which they are seen. But if I err in my judgment it will not be because I wish to treat the subject unfairly, or that I entertain any prejudice either for or against them. It must be borne in mind that I speak only of the Coolie or laboring classes, and of them as a body simply, without reference to individual exceptions. Before giving my own impressions of this class, however, let me give the reader a few quoted and

THE COOLIE'S HOME. — Page 131.

able opinions upon the race in general. The Rev. John L. Nevius, in his book upon China, says: * —

"The Chinese as a race are, as compared with European nations, of a phlegmatic and impassive temperament, and physically less active and energetic. Children are not fond of athletic and vigorous sports, but prefer marbles, kite-flying, and some quiet games of ball, spinning tops, etc. Men take an easy stroll for recreation, but never a rapid walk for exercise, and are seldom in a hurry or excited. They are also characteristically *timid and docile.* The oft-made assertion is probably true, that an army of ten or twenty thousand Europeans could march without serious opposition from one end of the Empire to the other. This remarkable disparity is, however, due principally to our knowledge of modern military science, and our possession of better warlike implements. Chinese well drilled, with confidence in their leaders and in each other, and equipped with modern fire-arms, would form an army which it would not be prudent to oppose with a force very inferior in numbers; though I have no doubt that with the same training and advantages they would still be found inferior to Europeans as soldiers.

"But while the Chinese are *deficient in active courage and daring,* they are not in passive re-

* "China and the Chinese," p. 278.

sistance. They are comparatively apathetic as regards pain and death, and have great powers of physical endurance as well as great persistency and obstinacy. On an average a Chinese tailor will work on his bench, or a literary man over books or with his pen, more hours a day than our race can.

"Physical development and strength and longevity vary in different parts of the empire. In and about Canton, from which we have derived the most of our impressions of China, as well as in most parts of the South, the people are small in stature, but in the Province of Shautung in the North, men varying in height from five feet eight inches to six feet are very common, while some of them are considerably taller, indeed, almost giants in stature. In this part of China I have known laborers over seventy years of age working daily at their trade, and it is not unusual to hear of persons who have reached the age of ninety or more. Other local peculiarities, physical and mental, need not be specially dwelt upon.

"The intellectuality of the Chinese is made evident by so many obvious and weighty facts that it seems strange that persons of ordinary intelligence and information should ever have questioned it. On this point it is better to state facts than individual opinions. We have before us a system of government and code of laws which will bear favorable comparison with those of Europeon nations, and have elicited a generous tribute of admiration and praise from our most competent and reliable writers. The practical wisdom and foresight of those who constructed this system are evinced by the fact that it has stood the test of time; enduring longer than any other which man has devised during the world's history; that it has bound together under one common rule a population to which the world affords no parallel, and given a degree of prosperity and of wealth which may challenge our wonder. Notwithstanding the rebellious and political agitations which have marked the history of this people, such has been their character and the vital and recuperative energy of the ideas into which they have been educated, that these disasters have been but temporary impediments in the continuous growth and development of the Empire. It is intelligent thought which has given China such a prominence in the East, and also in the eyes of Christendom. She may well point with pride to her authentic history, reaching back through more than thirty centuries; to her extensive literature, containing many works of sterling and permanent value; to her thoroughly elaborated language, possessed of a remarkable power of expression; to her list of scholars and her proficiency in belles-lettres. If these do not constitute evidences of intellectuality, it would be difficult to say where such evidence is to be found or on what basis we ourselves will rest our claim to intellectual superiority."

After severely lecturing the Europeans in China, and the Americans in particular, he speaks of the morality of the Chinese in this wise: "I have met with some of the most beautiful instances of affection, attachment, and gratitude in China which I have ever known. It has been my privilege to form the acquaintance of not a few Chinese whom I regard with more than ordinary affection and respect on account of the natural amiability of their dispositions, their sterling integrity and thorough Christian principle and devotion." *

The Rev. Justus Doolittle † says that "the Chinese at Foochau are shorter than the generality of foreigners, mild in character, and timid in appearance. They are not as turbulent, bloodthirsty, and daring as are the Chinese of some of the more southern sections of the Empire.‡ They indulge oftentimes in angry scolding and violent quarrelling in the streets, but seldom come to earnest blows. They are proud, self-relying, and look with disdain on foreigners."

* It will be observed that the writer refers to the Chinese in general, which includes the higher and refined classes, from whom he would naturally take his impressions.

† "Social Life of the Chinese."

‡ Referring to Kwangtung and Fukieu, no doubt, from whence came nearly all the immigrants in California.

Whatever difference of opinion may be entertained about their intellectual ability, or with regard to individual integrity, there can be but little controversy over the statement that Pride, Fear, and Cunning are the most prominent features of the Coolie's character. They pride themselves on their ancestry, no matter whether they were boatmen, mule-drivers, or beggars by the roadside; and any reflection upon the high standing of these relatives would make a secret enemy of the son at once. They pride themselves upon their family with all the relations, and the quickest way to stop a domestic quarrel is to say something derogatory to one or the other of the contestants. They will then embrace and at once turn their united forces upon the reviler. They pride themselves upon their features, and any race that differs from them is ugly and unattractive. They pride themselves on their dress, and even the best educated glory in a new gown or a new pair of shoes with all the simplicity of a child. They are proud of their nation, and while it abuses and oppresses them they never speak ill of it. They strut about with a haughty air when they have overreached a foreigner, or have beaten him in some competitive game, and arrogate to themselves great importance upon the least occasion. Fortunately the early philosophers who gave to China a standard of morality, and whose intellectual ability and goodness of heart were wonderful for that age, placed the standard high enough to make it worth competing for; so that he who reaches it in practice may well pride himself upon his position. The standard having been set and recognized by the natural teachings of the heart, this proud race pride themselves on every act that tends toward its morality. Thousands, ay all, practice morality out of regard to the speech of men. It is a feat to be moral in every respect, and to this idea is due much of their integrity in business and in keeping their plighted word. If the Coolie in China makes a promise to a neighbor he will try to keep it "though the heavens fall." Should he borrow money and verbally agree to pay it at a certain date, he will sell everything he has, even to his wife and children, to pay it. If he finds that he cannot pay, he will go and deliver himself up to the creditor to be sold as a slave, that the debt may be cancelled and no one have it to say that he did not keep his word. If he hires out as a servant he prides himself on doing his work as well as he has agreed to do, and a word of commendation for his honesty or integrity will make him true in the future, if he has not been in the past. Make him proud to serve you, and no truer servant ever entered a household. Of course there are exceptions, and perhaps many of them, in European towns where "deeds of honor" are not looked upon with such favor, but I speak of them collectively as they appear in China. This pride prevents any change in their habits of life. They would be ashamed to undertake the introduction of a new custom and incur the ridicule of so doing. The old customs are the best, and he that can go through the old ceremony with the most grace has the greatest reason to pride himself on his fashionable accomplishments. When their circumstances are such that they take little pride in the practice of virtue, fear will serve to accomplish the same end. They are very timid, and seldom get sufficiently angry to overcome the fear of consequences. Fear, as has been stated enters largely into their religion, and they sacrifice often to the devil-gods and perform many arduous ceremonies to insure that deity's good-will, while they almost wholly neglect the benevolent and propitious gods to whom they are indebted for all their blessings. Their superstitions consist in a great part of omens of evil that work upon the fears. They dare not stir in defence of their rights under their own laws, and suffer almost incredible tortures rather than offend an officer of justice. They are afraid of every person occupying a higher station than themselves, and to all outward appearance would endure much privation rather than transgress his slightest will. With all their disrespect for foreigners, they are afraid of them, and the presence of a European bearing an official character seems to strike them with something like awe. I attribute their good order and laudable desire to learn to read as much to their perpetual fear of the Emperor's spies, whom they imagine to be all about them and reporting both their good and evil deeds directly to him, as to their personal pride.

They are also a deceitful and cunning people; and whenever they can transgress a custom or a statute without exposure to ridicule or the penalties of law, I think they would not hesitate to do it, provided they were to gain anything by so doing. They dare not take much risk, and they are cunning enough to know and weigh the chances. If they contemplate any unlawful deed, they will turn the subject over and over in their minds and look at it from all possible situations, before they make any move. A servant which a friend of mine employed in Hongkong, determined to steal his employer's penknife, which he saw one day lying on the writing-desk. Instead of taking it at once, he hid it under a bundle of movable paper, where it remained for two or three days. He then pretended to find it, and smilingly restored it to his thankful employer without waiting for any inquiry to be made about it; another time the servant took the knife from his employer's pocket while he slept, and although the owner was sure he had the knife in his pocket when he went to bed, yet he made up his mind that he did not, when he saw it lying open on his writing-desk the next morning. This was done to make him lose confidence in his own memory, and the first act to give him confidence in the integrity of his servant. Soon after the knife disappeared altogether, and, never doubting the honesty of his long-tried servant, the loser made up his mind that he had mislaid it as "he had done once before." The knife coming into my hands through a pawnbroker, it was recognized by my friend, and its transfer was traced back through several parties to the servant, and the whole story confessed.

The policy of the government in its intercourse with foreign nations shows this same spirit of pride, fear, and cunning. Had it been bold and less proud, depending on the justice of its proposals rather than on the secret policy which they covered, China, and I may say the whole world, would have been much benefited by our diplomatic intercourse.

Not denying but that the Coolies have love, hate, patriotism, and all the other various passions which characterize the human race, yet the three peculiarities mentioned overrule and partially hide the others. There are instances in which they have shown the deepest affection for friends and where they have been disinterestedly generous. There are cases of bravery on record of which any nation might be proud. But after a candid and careful consideration I am obliged to consider these cases as exceptions. They treat their women as slaves, and have no regard for female virtue. They show little or no real love for their children, and act very much as I have seen some husbands in huts equally dirty in the suburbs of European cities. It may be that tyranny and privation have made them brutish, and that in a healthier political atmosphere their expiring affections will again burn bright. I hope so.

Their regard for their old mothers and fathers has often been cited as an instance of remarkable affection among these laborers, and it does at first sight seem to be a commendable virtue. But when we consider it as a part of their religious duty which is enforced with threats of vengeance from the gods, and understand how this superstitious fear is the only thing that can overcome their pride and cunning, or make them rebel, we can see a powerful motive for this show of respect, which takes away one half of its romantic interest. For the honor, pride, and satisfaction of having this respect paid her when she gets old, the mother who would otherwise drown or strangle her infant will tend upon it and rear it to womanhood. This strange lack of the finer feelings of humanity may seem unaccountable to the reader who has known only the ways and thoughts of civilized men, and somewhat startling perhaps to the observer of the Chinese under their improved conditions in California. For only in his own land can the heathen be seen in his natural state. Living an aimless life, possessing nothing but a family, knowing little or no intellectual enjoyment, and like a beast of burden dragging, dragging, dragging out the long dull days thinking only of eating, sleeping, and clothing himself and family. He has nothing to call out his higher instincts, and it is not his fault if he is beastly in his ways and appearance. It must be borne in mind that I am writing of the classes who emigrate, and not of the middle, educated, or higher classes. The Coolie is but a broken, unseemly reflection of the higher classes. If they respect America, *he* will never show disrespect. If they believe in traditions, and tell him of it, he will, in his rude way, believe in them too. A kind of lower strata which can only be raised by taking it out from under the oppressive layers that weigh it down. Who shall do it? That is a question for statesmen.

The Chinese seem to be wonderfully endowed by nature, and I think owe their disposition and present condition more to peculiar circumstances than to any natural deficiency. In all departments of labor they are able, after a very short tutorage, to work at the side of any European. Their patience and caution is as wonderful as their ready wit. Lacking an inventive mind, — owing perhaps to the fact that there has been nothing in China to encourage invention, — they are able to copy or imitate anything which they have ever seen performed. The stories about their making a new coat and burning a hole in it because there was one in the sample, and of breaking off a shoe-nail in just the same place on the sole where they saw their employer break one accidentally, as well as their setting up of books and papers without being able to read a word of print, are too old to be repeated here, but show the whole tendency of the Chinese mind. They print Bibles, make steam-engines, or cook a meal with the same readiness, provided they have seen it done. They must have been inventive once, or whence came the knowledge of the compass, of gunpowder, of weaving, and of water-clocks? It would seem that just as the nation was making most gigantic strides towards civilization it became paralyzed; and for the last two thousand years it has been doing nothing but living over the past; while within the last twelve or fifteen years it has made a perceptible step downwards.

> "Ill fares the land, to hastening ills a prey,
> Where wealth accumulates, and men decay."

I cannot avoid picturing to myself what China

might be, with a liberal and civilized imperial government. How with its rich unworked mines of gold, iron, and copper,— its fertile valleys and broad arable plains all improved,—its great waterfalls turned into manufacturing uses,—with a people so shrewd and skilful to work them,—and with a government strong enough to hold them together while they learned to govern themselves, — it might be the greatest nation of the earth in everything that makes wealth, power, or happiness. But this will never be until the blinding religion of Boodah and the rationalistic theories of Confucius are replaced by the cheering and enlightening religion of Jesus Christ.

It has been supposed by many that they were the most patriotic people on the face of the whole earth. This idea has doubtless arisen from the exhibitions of national pride to be found among the higher classes, and the universal desire of emigrants to be carried back when they die and be buried in their native soil. The latter fact, however, is owing much more to their superstition than to their love for the land or its institutions. They have an idea,—the Coolies more especially, —that somehow the spirit lingers near the body or flits back and forth between the grave and the lettered tablet set up to be worshipped in the kitchen of his relations. They also believe that certain localities are lucky and certain others unlucky, and that a well-made grave with plenty of burning joss-sticks will often ward off the evils of an unlucky locality. If the body of a deceased parent or relative is buried in a very fortunate locality — one that is blessed by the presence of an imaginary spirit of luck, called *Fung Shwuy* — they believe that this propitious circumstance will build up the fortunes of his family by making it learned, wealthy, and numerous. Great care is taken in China in the selection of cemeteries, and no burial will be made on a spot until some peculiar circumstance has indicated that Fung Shwuy has a good opinion of it. As the Chinaman feels that after death he will be dependent upon his living relatives for "mock money" to make his purchases while in purgatory, and that he will need their intercession to secure his choice of bodies as his next spiritual abode, he is careful to select a burial-place which will give his descendants or relatives good fortune, — making the performance of a filial duty serve a selfish purpose. In foreign lands he has no choice of burial-places, and does not feel sure but that, even should he select one and be buried in a lucky locality, his body may be removed by some heartless foreigner before his spirit is clear of purgatory and consequent ruin be brought upon his family and himself. The idea that the whole family are participators in whatever good or ill luck the Gods vouchsafe to any

one of them seems to keep families together, and to make them much more careful of each other than would be the case did these relations depend upon their dulled natural affections.

This selfish interest which each family has in its members is the cause of their clannishness, which in case of clan-quarrels results in such horrible feuds and blood-chilling deeds. Bound for his own safety to protect his relatives, and having more fear of the Hereafter than of present suffering or death, the Coolie, often through superstitious fear, does deeds of valor that, in a land less fanatical would pass current as the bravest acts ever prompted by affection. So that, while his strong desire to be buried at home with his kindred and on his native soil strikes us at first as being prompted by love and patriotism, yet his action is much more the result of his cowardly heathen fears. Far be it from me to belittle their virtues or to explain away any evidence which would in truth establish their title to generosity or moral worth. The public demand candid, unprejudiced opinions, and such has careful afterthought established these to be. Those who have studied the deadening influences of heathen religion on the descendants of families once civilized, and have marked how tyranny kills the life of the affections, and makes brutes of men naturally kind and generous, will pity the Chinaman rather than blame him for his lack of refinement. A good evidence of the existence of other motives than that of patriotism is found in the fact that it is seldom the Chinese in the colonies of Singapore or Penang send home the bodies of the dead. They have secured from the English authorities a permanent title to a "lucky" locality, and, although they claim to be Chinamen still, and are surrounded by foreigners, yet deem it no hardship to be interred there. The proximity of their family and the propitious circumstances for which their strange faith calls, is all they want, and the idea that they think there is any special virtue in the soil or atmosphere of China is at once exploded. Surely they are a strange people, exhibiting a remarkable degree of natural talent; which, however, is so stunted, marred, and misdirected by custom and religion, that, like the vine which climbs the barren and shady side of a rocky cliff, it twists into the queerest shapes, — beats back and forth between wind and rock, battering its leaves and destroying its fruit, — a gnarled, unseemly scrag.

CHAPTER IV.

THIRST FOR GOLD.

Poverty of the Coolie. — Official Extortion. — The Effect upon the Laborer's Character. — Lack of Avariciousness. — Behavior in California. — Eating Rats and Dogs. — Selling Females and destroying Infants.

AN entire chapter has been reserved for the discussion of the avaricious element in the Chinese character, because of the almost universal opinion that a natural "thirst for gold" has been the only influence animating the hearts of voluntary immigrants from China. It is so natural to suppose that others are moved by the same desires and passions which animate us! When we see men treating their parents with respect and acting kindly toward their brothers, sisters, and children, it is almost a shock to be told that it is not done as "a spontaneous outpouring of a loving heart." We look from our lofty civilization down upon a heathen race, supposing that they feel as we do; not realizing that circumstances have cast them in a different mould, nor that their springs of action are founded on far different motives. So, we suppose, because we left our homes and all the luxuries of life, to endure hardships unnumbered, and encounter dangers most horrid, with the hope of enriching ourselves in the new gold-mines of California, that the Chinese, who have no luxuries to leave, must have come there for the same purpose. The fact of their being found there, working diligently in the mines, is *prima facie* evidence that gold-hunting was the sole object for which they came; but it is by no means conclusive evidence.

The experiences of the laborers in China would seem to make the love of money (they have no gold) much stronger in their breasts than in those of other nationalities. Certainly there is no country, not excepting Syria, where the lower classes suffer so much on its account. Reference has already been made to the governmental extortions and to the universal system of bribery. Let me enumerate further. The Coolie laborer in China receives in the agricultural districts eight or ten dollars a year, with his own board. Out of this eight or ten dollars he must provide for his family and clothe himself. If his family is large it will cost six dollars to clothe them, and more than the balance to board them. Only think of it! in a family of six there would be but a dollar's worth

of clothing for each during the year, and about sixty cents' worth of food. But wait! They do not get so much as that. His "per capita" tax is eighty cents, and his tablets, &c. for regular worship will be a dollar, and his rent will be two dollars. This amounts to three dollars and eighty cents. Then, if he gets ten dollars a year, and avoids all extra calls upon his purse, he will have only six dollars and twenty cents left for the support of his family and clothing himself during a whole year. Now, if he injure or break an implement he will be charged for that; and it would be strange if in the course of a year he escaped without a single accident! His relatives may die and he be assessed for a share, if not for the whole, of the funeral expenses. In cases of rebellion, — and they happen nearly every year, — an extra tax is collected to defray the governmental expenses; while he may, in case of drought, be thrown out of work entirely. Carpenters and masons get about twenty-two cents a day, boarding themselves, but their taxes are sufficient to bring their income down to an equality with the farm hands. Clerks get twelve or fifteen dollars a year and their board. It must be said, in justice to the employers, that the Coolie usually gets his wages — such as they are — promptly. Sometimes the women assist somewhat in the support of the family, but unless they are sufficiently robust to endure field labor,

their income will not be more than four or five dollars a year, they boarding themselves. Now, in order to live upon their wages and pay their taxes and assessments, they are obliged to adopt a thousand expedients for making palatable what would otherwise be offensive, and to live on the very coarsest food. In some districts they pay out two thirds of their wages in taxes, in which case they must find, beg, or steal their food for the whole year. Now it would seem that these circumstances, if there was nothing more, would be sufficient to give them an uncontrollable greed for money. But the best part only of the story has now been told. They seldom in these latter years escape assessment to the full amount of their wages; if not in one shape, it comes in another. They are constantly getting in debt. They are arrested for fictitious misdemeanors and fined by the avaricious mandarin, and on stating their inability to pay him, are given a "week to make return," which means go and steal it or be whipped and put in the stocks. They are incited to quarrel by the members of other families, for the purpose of furnishing an excuse to "capture" them and sell them to Portuguese traders. They are bled by false doctors, who want to sell the blood to alchemists. Their teeth are pulled to make salable trinkets. They are often punished, together with their whole village, for the act of some man who has escaped.

They are accused of many crimes which their superiors have committed and laid to their charge. Often do they die of fatigue in the hot rice-fields, live a lingering death, afflicted with loathsome disease, or drown themselves in the creeks and rivers, for the want of a few cash with which to buy the necessaries of life. "Money! money!" cry the half-starved children. "Money!" pleads his wretched wife. "Money!" call the spirits of discontented and poverty-stricken ancestors at the bars of Hades. "Money!" calls the village elder. "Money!" demands the lessee of his hovel. "Money!" thunders the Emperor. "Money!" shouts the mandarian in the halls of *in*justice. If the Coolie work day and night, the cash is called for many times before it is earned. He suffers all kinds of injustice himself, and knows that his is the general condition of his class: lying, stealing, cheating, robbing, extorting, maiming, murdering, are going on all the while within the circle of his limited acquaintance, — all for money. He sees the elder, the mandarin, the governor, and even the Emperor, pardoning the perpetrators of these crimes, — all for money. He hears the thunder of English guns, sees cities burning and men and women torn, bleeding, and dying, that opium may be introduced, which will steal away what little humanity there is left. What is it all for? *Money.* These things, taken together with his belief that with money he could secure eternal bliss, not only for himself but for all his family, ancestry and posterity, would in a European breast awaken such a thirst for money that neither friend nor foe, hardship nor death would stand in the way of its possession.

Dr. Williams well understood the state of society with relation to this matter as early as 1849, when he wrote his excellent work. It has grown worse since. He said then that "one natural consequence of such a state of society, and such a perversion of justice, is to render the people afraid of all contact with the officers of government and exceedingly selfish in all their intercourse, though the latter trait needs no particular training to develop it in any heathen country. It also tends to an inhuman disregard of the life of others and chills every emotion of kindness which might otherwise arise."

Let us turn from the result which might be if the Chinese were like Europeans, to the result which is. For, instead of creating such a "thirst for gold" among the Coolies as we would most naturally expect, it seems to have lessened its value. In the districts about Canton they seem to have lost all care for anything more than mere existence. This disregard for money would be interpreted to be the result of so much hardship and so little encouragement did it not show itself, though in a modified form — in the open ports. At present there is a very large number of Chinese in Hongkong, where they are governed by the English authorities, and nearly all employed by European merchants. There they have a right to their own time and to make their own bargains. In some departments there is a great demand for skilled labor and but a small supply. Yet such laborers work for nearly the same pay as those whose departments are crowded. They might "strike," — as they sometimes do in the interior, and often with bloody results, — but they show little disposition to do it in Hongkong. They get fair wages and are satisfied. Not but that they would take more if it came in their way, but their avariciousness does not make them uneasy with what they receive. The usual result of raising a person's pay in Europe is an expectation on his part that the employer will repeat the action in a few days. There have been "strikes" even among the well-educated workmen of America, resulting directly from an advance made in their wages. They believe, and in some localities consistently enough, that the first advance is an example worthy of frequent imitation. But the Chinaman works on year after year for the same wages, perfectly contented unless some one offers him more. He lays by what he can spare of his wages, and, be it little or more, is generally contented. Persons who have had Chinamen in their employ at San Francisco tell me that two servants have worked for months side by side, one getting sixteen dollars and another twenty-five, showing no ill-feeling, — and doing the same work. This was because the employer did not wish for two servants, and would not give the second one more wages to keep him. Meantime no effort was made on the part of the poorly paid servant to find another and more lucrative position. It is a noted fact that the Chinamen in the mines were perfectly content to work on poorly paying lodes close alongside of the richest veins in the district. They worked the mine, too, as long as they found anything valuable, and were not, like their civilized companions, jumping about from claim to claim in hope of doing better. In case they found a rich vein of gold, and, as was rarely the case, were permitted to remain on it, they were exceedingly pleased at their good fortune; but it did not make them as uneasy and important as the same luck did the Americans. It was not often that they worked a rich mine if they found it; for they were too much afraid of the white miners to be seen where gold was plenty, and cunning enough to perceive that the too great accumulation of dust would result in the loss of the whole by theft or robbery. Yet these things did not disturb their temper or industry; and they worked on, every day laying up

THE TREE GOD. — Page 136.

something, and in some cases getting to be very wealthy. This same spirit has characterized their action wherever they have been employed. They do not expect the same wages which an American gets for the same work. They find no fault if it is much less, provided the employer keeps his contract. This is the general rule at present, to which, of course, there are exceptions.

Connected with this subject is the statement that the Chinamen live upon rats, dogs, vermin, &c., in order to hoard up the money which decency would oblige them to spend for proper food. While it is true that he is in the habit of saving every particle of food which he does not need, and seldom expends his money in confections or pastry, it is also true that the Coolie provides himself and family with wholesome food whenever he has the means to do so. To this there may also be exceptions, but they are few indeed. They take pride in living respectably, both in regard to food and clothing, and I have yet to hear of an instance where the Coolie's pride, unchecked by fear, did not overcome any miserly sentiments he had acquired. The laborers in California may deprive themselves of the necessities of life in order to send money home to pay their debts or provide for their families, as they would more naturally take pride in so doing than in having a costly table among the "barbarians."

I have no doubt but that the poor, oppressed Coolie in China often eats rats and dogs, and even more disgusting food, for the very good reason that he would starve if he did not, although no such food has ever been brought to my notice. I have tasted of some *doubtful* dishes at the table of Chinese gentlemen, both in California and China, and suppose the laborer to be even less refined in his tastes. His condition would naturally make him so. But it is evident that rats, cats, dogs, &c. are never eaten from choice. In the colonies and seaports, where the Coolie escapes the extortions of interior officers, and gets average wages, such a thing is never known. Yet dogs are so plenty as to be a nuisance, and as for the cats, there would be a thousand thankful hearts if the Chinamen *would* dispose of them and their horrid night yawling, by eating or otherwise. Rats also revel in luxury and security around the wharves, warehouses, and dwellings in seaports, and I have seen a parcel of Coolies having the liveliest sport in trying to catch one which they had surrounded in the middle of the street. But when they had killed it they threw it off the dock into the sea and went about their business as a crowd of Europeans would do under the same circumstances. I have seen floating in the harbors the bodies of cats and dogs which had been drowned by the boatmen, — the lowest class of Chinese, — for

the purpose of getting rid of them; owing to the animal's old age or the accidental fracture of a limb. If their love for money was sufficiently strong to cause them to eat such animals in the interior, where to possess money is to be a mark for every official extortion, they certainly would practise it where this kind of food was plenty, and themselves safe from robbery.

Two things at least in the Chinese customs I have found worthy of praise. First, their neat preparation of food; and second, the exemption of their literature from every obscene word or reference. It has been shown, by the introduction of paintings and vile pamphlets by unscrupulous sailors, that the sale of such works might be a profitable business; yet no Chinaman would be seen engaged in it. His scruples, however, seldom extend into practical life, showing that his pride in sustaining a moral standard, although he does not pretend to live up to it, is greater than this "thirst for gold."

The sale of girls for doubtful purposes, and the killing of female infants, has been cited as an evidence of their lust for wealth. To which I can only reply, in law phrase, *necessitate non leges* (necessity knows no law); and adding simply my opinion that the cases where either is done, without abject poverty for their excuse, are *less frequent* among them than they are in civilized communities, I pass to a more interesting, if not more important, topic.

CHAPTER V.

EARLY EMIGRATION.

Settlement of Borneo. — The Colonization of Singapore. — How the Coolies obtained Wives. — The Effect of Chinese Labor. — Filthy Homes. — The City of Penang. — A Description of the Market Street.

THE Chinese are very far from being a migratory people. Their natural love for home and country is stronger than that of any other race on earth, and when they turn their backs upon their native land, it is for a more powerful motive than would be necessary to influence a European in taking the same step. They have, nevertheless, emigrated in small numbers from time to time, and have established several flourishing colonies.

As early as the Chow dynasty (1100 B. C.) a body of Chinese are said to have settled in Borneo, and when that island was discovered by the Portuguese (1526 A. D.) they were practically, though not nominally, the rulers and law-makers. There is no evidence of their making any great improvements, or of their undertaking such enterprises as distinguished their countrymen at home. Their natural shrewdness being far superior to that of the Bujis and Malayans, they were able without war to keep such a control of the island as to turn its valuable productions into commercial account. Pearls, diamonds, iron, copper, and tin, as well as the fruits for which the island is at present noted, were imported into China from these colonies as early as 800 B. C. This Chinese colony consisted of men who brought their families and permanently settled; practising there all the customs and ceremonies which they had known in China.

What was the cause for their expatriation can only be conjectured. Some say, "hope of gain in a commercial view"; others that they were pirates, who made the island a rendezvous; while the most consistent view which I have heard is taken by Father Bado, a Catholic missionary, who states that they were guilty parties who, with their families, were banished for life. At present they have a much less pleasing figure in the eyes of the traveller than the Cantonese, and in some parts of the island have so far amalgamated with the native races that no person of pure Chinese blood is seen among them. Several other islands off the coast of China, including Formosa and Celebes, have been visited from time to time by Chinese colonists; but they were either exterminated by the natives, returned to China, or, as has happened, amalgamated with those barbarous, bloodthirsty pirates, whose deeds have been a terror to the navigators of Chinese waters for the last five hundred years. No colonies, however, whose history has any direct bearing upon the question now agitating this country were established until 1824 or 1825.* Then a large number of Chinese were induced by the English merchants of Singapore (Malacca) to make that island their temporary home, and engage in the manufacture of rope mats, &c., for the China market. Their industry and skill obtained for them permanent employment, and as the town grew in importance the number of Chinamen was augmented. Finally, a part of the city site was given them for building-spots.

When the number had increased to several thousand, a ship-load of prostitutes was brought down from Macaow as a matter of speculation. These were followed by others, until "Chinese town" was filled with them. The attention of the English authorities being called to the subject, and the Chinese fearing the removal of their mistresses, took them in marriage according to the custom of China. The laws of their own country forbids marriages that have not been arranged by the parents, but do not make invalid such a marriage after it is made. So these Chinamen, although some of them doubtless had one or more wives in

* Mongolia and Manchuria are not properly Chinese colonies.

China, were nevertheless legal husbands, and their wives exclusively their own. As for the character of the woman it has no weight with a Chinaman of the laboring class, as virtue in woman seems to be of no consequence to him. From these marriages sprung up a generation of children who have since intermarried among themselves, and who know no other home.

It was stated to me by priests who had resided there for twenty-five years, that not a single legal wife from China had ever been brought to Singapore. If so, the law against the emigration of wives must be more strictly enforced than is that against the departure of men. A wife being considered a piece of property, to be used for profit or pleasure, and even sold at the will of the husband, he would most assuredly attempt to obtain her, if by so doing he did not incur too great a risk. However that may be, there are plenty of women now in the colony, and, judging by the number of dirty children seen running about, one would suppose the prospects of growth to be excellent indeed. They already number over thirty thousand, and by their labor the Europeans have built one of the finest cities in the East. They cut the timber, make the brick, and build the houses. They lay out and pave the streets and quays. They man ships, transfer cargoes, and cultivate twenty-five thousand acres of adjacent land.

They sell many thousand dollars' worth of pepper, cocoanuts, pine-apples, nutmegs, mace, cloves, ginger, fruit, and sugar. They charm the poisonous serpents, kill the tigers, porcupines, and wild-cats. Act as street inspectors, clerks, bookkeepers, shoemakers, tailors, barbers, merchants, compradors, money-changers, hackmen, footmen, cooks, house-servants; and one, whom I saw before a lazy set of native Malayans, was preaching the Gospel of Christ. The Malayans do considerable work and a great deal of stealing and cheating, so that the advantage of their labor is counterbalanced by the disadvantage of their duplicity; while the Chinese, more perhaps on account of their hereditary respect for authority and fear of the law than their love for truth or honesty, are faithful in the fulfilment of contracts and careful of their employers' interests. This view of their character gives to the Chinese colonist an attractive air, which his countrymen at home possess only in a much smaller degree.

There is another characteristic which makes a far different impression. They take good care of their own persons, but their houses, children, cats, and dogs are filthy in the extreme. The stench about their dwellings is almost unendurable to a European, and the cesspools and slimy ditches in their backyards would breed the cholera in the most salubrious climate in the world. While the

Chinaman is cleansing the house of his employer and removing every particle of dirt with scrupulous care, his family at home are living in the most slovenly quarters, where vermin of a hundred species revel in luxurious nastiness. How they can go from neat stores or fine drawing-rooms where they are employed, to eat and sleep in those foul quarters, is a mystery which I have yet to hear explained. Notwithstanding their neglect of tidiness at home, they are a valuable, and in that locality an indispensable, part of the population. Europeans could not do the labor in that hot climate, and the logy Malayans would not.

The colony at Penang, on the Prince of Wales Island (Malacca), originated some years later, but in about the same way as did that at Singapore, and was made permanent by nearly the same means. It numbers about sixteen thousand, and occupies a town separate and apart from the English settlement. Here they are allowed to conduct their own affairs without fear of interference from the European authorities, unless they should see fit to organize a raid or a rebellion, in which case the English troops would be called out. They have their own officers, settle their own difficulties, and make their own contracts.

A visit to their village was one of the most interesting episodes in my recent "trip around the world." It is situated about a mile from the Port, and the main road leading to the celebrated Penang waterfalls forms the principal street. The houses were built of brick and wood, with dark red tiles for roofing, such as are found everywhere in China, and in some European cities. They were a story and a half high, and all built together, so that the gable-end of one house answered the purpose of two, and was also the partition between the apartments of different owners. The first story of each having the front room entirely open to the street, gave to the town the appearance of long rows of sheds.

Over and about them, almost hiding the roofs, and arching the street, hung the luxuriant foliage of a tropical forest, like a loosely braided mat of green from which stared huge bunches of green cocoanuts and long clusters of yellow bananas. Mangoes and mangosteens lay partially hid under the great leaves of the palm, while the perfume of orange-blossoms and cinnamon-buds sweetened the air until each inhalation seemed to be a draught fit for the gods. Flowers! O, such colors! They hung on the roofs, peeped out of cracks, sprang up about the door-way, filled the pots which the merchant placed on his show-case or platform, and shone in the sunlight among the leaves and vine-covered branches of the nutmeg-tree. Nearly every front room was used as a shop, for the exposure and sale of merchandise. The bunches of bananas and grapes, cocoanuts and figs, apples and cherries of the fruit-dealer hung in artistically arranged rows over his head, while melons, berries, peaches, dates, and a dozen strange varieties of tropical fruit lay in the show-boxes, on the platforms around him. The dealer in vegetables in the next stall was barricaded with cucumbers, yams, sweet-potatoes, pumpkins, onions, garlic, short pieces of sugar-cane, ginseng, gourds, tomatoes, and plantains, — piled up before him in tiny heaps, and hung in bamboo-tied bunches all about his head. Next comes a dealer in wild animals, which he keeps in unpleasant proximity to the street, and behind treacherous-looking bars of chestnut and bamboo. The presence of a stranger arouses the monkey and his companion, — the wild man from Borneo, — and they screech and scratch until they arouse the tiger, and bring an ominous growl from the box where can be seen the half-exposed paw of a lion. Then begins an awful din from a dozen boxes in the farther apartment, where the leopards, dogs, foxes, and great snakes are confined, and the European beholder, unless he is very anxious for a trade, will scarcely wait for new exhibitions of their rage.

Next the bird-shop with its discordant jangle of parrot whistles, nightingale chirrups, canary peeps, hen chuckles, and lark twitters, calls us in as far as we can get to see the bright plumage of the birds of India and China. So we go; along the street, around the rice, maize, and barley boxes of the grain-dealer, by the piles of cotton and rolls of silk and fine shawls exposed by the dry-goods merchant, stopping to see the money-changer count his cash by means of big sliding beads hung on a stick, and hurrying past the tailors, the weavers, the blacksmiths, the shoemakers, the temples of Boodah, to visit the gardens which are said to be hidden by the trees. What a change it is! to go from the tidy, well-swept street in front to the dirty, rubbish-encumbered back yard! How bad the filth might appear, were it not for the rich foliage of the trees overhead that attracts the eye, or how offensive its odors might seem, did not the spice-trees drown it with sweetness, I will not venture to say. Away through the trees by the hencoops and dog-kennels we go, until a brilliant light ahead shows us the opening.

There are the gardens! How the stall-keepers in Fulton or Quincy markets would stare to see these immense cabbages and bursting onions! Corn above one's head, carrot-tops knee high, peas and potatoes that look like pumpkin-vines, and turnips that appear, when pulled, like squashes with tops! I have visited boasted gardens in the South and West of the United States, seen prize productions in many European lands, but this Chinese garden leads them all. Not a weed or an unthrifty plant. Everything trained and propped to keep it in harmony with the general design. But neither the visitor nor reader can tarry long, so we hurry back through the trees, — into a back room, where a Chinese mother on a mat is teaching a little girl to sew, — out through the toy and curio shop, into the street, which has filled with long-cued, blue-gowned gentry, anxious to see the carriage. With a cheerful "*To-tsa Ni-tso-shan,*" — "Many thanks; good morning to you!" — we shoot along the smooth road, — out of the village, — into the cocoanut forest, — toward that sheening, leaping waterfall so much like Yosemite.

As far as the Penang and Singapore colonies are concerned, there can be said to be but little difference between the habits, customs, or religious faith of the Chinese there and in China. They live at peace with the Malayans, Indiamen, and Europeans, provide for their own poor, and appear to be getting rich. They seem, however, to have lost all inclination to return to China, which proves to my satisfaction that the desire for return or for burial in China, strong as it is, can be entirely overcome under auspicious circumstances.

CHAPTER VI.

A NEW CHAPTER OF HORRORS.

The Beginning of the "Coolie Trade." — The first Cargo. — How procured. — Wholesale Man-stealing. — Interference of civilized Nations. — Regulations to prevent Kidnapping. — Table of the Number of Coolie Slaves. — What has become of the immense Number taken to Cuba and Peru.

EARLY in the spring of the year 1847 a square-rigged vessel of eight hundred tons came into the port of Macaow, China, with a cargo of groceries and specie. She was a Portuguese craft named "Don Pedro," and hailed from the port of Lisbon. It was the intention of the captain to exchange the incoming cargo for tea and silk, which he supposed to be awaiting his arrival. He found, however, that he must wait several weeks for the cargo, as the crop of tea had not begun to come in. This was a little annoying to the impatient skipper, and in expressing himself rather strongly one day in the counting-room of the assignees of his cargo, he was reproved by a senior partner of the firm, and a quarrel with blows ensued. This cost the captain his charter, and he was obliged to look about for some other merchandise. While canvassing for a cargo, he fell in with a Spaniard, fresh from Peru, who had come over to settle some long-standing accounts between himself as a sugar-dealer and a number of the firms in Macaow. The Spaniard was surprised with the cheapness of labor in China, and incidentally wished that he had a thousand Chinese in Peru. This led to the discussion of the expediency of taking the Chinese to Peru, and finally to an attempt on their part to load the "Don Pedro" with Coolies. This they did under the pretence of shipping them for Java; but whether any contracts were made with these men is not at present known. They obtained three hundred Coolies, for whose passage the Spaniard became responsible. Near the first day of June the "Don Pedro" sailed out of the port of Macaow with three hundred as happy men as ever trod the planks of a ship. Believing the falsehoods that had been told them, and expecting soon to return to their homes wealthier men, they looked back upon the disappearing shores, sighing only for the time when they should see them again. It is doubtful if any one of them has yet seen their native land, and as doubtful that any of them ever will do so. After one hundred days of storm, exposed to cold and heat, with half rations and but little water, one hundred and seventy-five were landed at a port near Callao, to be treated even worse on land than they had been on the sea. The Spaniard swore to his own story, and no one could understand the Chinaman's complaint, if he had any to make. They were put on a plantation in the interior where they could not run away, and the experiment of Coolie labor tried for the first time in that state. It was satisfactory to the contractor, and another cargo was sent for. Coming to the ears of planters in Cuba, who knew that in a few months they must part with their slaves, they also sent ships to bring over the Chinese. The story of the successful Coolie traffic soon spread over the Spanish and Portuguese dominions, and Peru, Australia, Surinam, and the Indian Archipelago vied with Cuba in the traffic of human labor. But it was not to be expected that many cargoes of voluntary emigrants could be procured when it was found that the time for the return of the first shipload had passed, with no news from the husbands and fathers who left in the "Don Pedro." Besides this, rumors began to be afloat that the Coolies were taken to "the other side of the world" to be enslaved for a series of years and finally murdered. When the ships which followed the "Don Pedro" on her second visit arrived at Macaow, the Chinese were too much alarmed to be induced by any offers to go on board. Then began that system of kidnapping, purchasing, chaining, starving, and, as it may appropriately be called, *murdering*, which for twenty years shocked the feelings of all humane persons and cast a dark blot upon the Portuguese and Spanish escutcheons that can never be expunged. Fathers and mothers sold their sons, fugitives bargained away themselves, banditti brought in their male and female prisoners and sold them in lots to the traders, for which sums never exceeding ten dollars per person were thankfully received. The market being ill supplied with purchasable human beings, the traders organized bands of night-thieves, whose business it was to steal into the cabins of the laborers and carry on board the ship the father and sons, and sometimes the whole family. Although these bands were numerous, and Coolies were captured by the thousand, still the demand increased beyond their kidnapping capacity. Then ships called "Lorchas" were manned and armed as if for war, and sent up the bays and rivers to fall suddenly upon the unsuspecting inhabitants of some rural district. This was a great success. In the face of the navies of the civilized world these pirate vessels carrying the Portuguese flag would enter some towns unperceived and capture whole cargoes at a single swoop. Old men were seized in the rice-fields, boys in the school-room, young men in the shops, and carried by force to the suffocating holds of the vessels at Macaow. The province of Quantung was filled with orphan children and the mourning-white was seen in nearly every household. Soon other ports followed the baleful example, and in the year 1853 Hongkong, Swatow, Canton, Amoy, Whampoa, Cumsing-Moon, and several other smaller ports, harbored vessels awaiting cargoes of these slaves.

It carried civil war into a hundred villages of Quantung. Rival clans and families took up arms against each other, and carried off the prisoners, to be sold to the Peruvian and Spanish traders. No better evidence of the inefficiency of the Chinese government need be presented than the behavior of the officials during the most prosperous years of the Coolie trade. The mandarins and village elders not only connived at the wholesale robbery, but for a small fee sent their personal attendants to assist in the capture and chaining of citizens belonging to their own town. If they had an enmity against any one, or felt that any man was a hindrance to their extortions, they took great care that he should be captured and sold to the slave-dealers in port. In 1854 the enormities committed by the Coolie traders came to the ears of the British government, and measures were immediately taken to prevent the further traffic in the port of Hongkong. British and German vessels were soon forbidden by their own governments to engage in the barbarous trade. The treatment of the Coolies on board ship and after their arrival at their destination seems, however, to have had more to do with the action of those powers than the force used in their capture. Such numbers were stowed into the vessels and such poor food given them that, notwithstanding their hardy manner of life at home, hundreds died on the voyages. After arriving at the Chincha Islands, or wherever else they were taken, they were treated in every way as slaves. They were tasked and whipped, made to work night and day, and given only sufficient food to sustain life, with no prospect — until after the interference of other nations — of ever being liberated. Many stabbed themselves with pieces of wood, or hung themselves to the masts of guano ships, while three hundred, in 1856, drowned themselves in the ocean during a single day off the Guano Islands near the coast of Peru. Out of the one hundred and fifty thousand taken to the Spanish and South American colonies, before the year 1865, it is doubtful if five hundred ever returned.

Sometimes it happened that the Coolies mutinied on board before the arrival of the vessels in port, and, failing to overcome the crews, they threw themselves overboard in a body. Several ships have been captured by Coolies, the crews butchered and the vessels sunk or abandoned near some island shore. One cargo of Coolies in 1857 murdered their captors, and knowing nothing of navigation cruised about until two hundred starved, and the vessel with the remainder grounded on the coast of the Feegee Islands. Several successful mutinies have occurred recently. In one case in 1867 the Coolies in their rage cut the bodies of the officers and crew into mince-meat, and are said to have eaten some of the pieces to allay their hunger. Three vessels with Coolies have never been heard from, four have been captured by the Coolies, and eight terribly bloody mutinies have been successfully quelled since 1852, of which there is record. How many more there may have been I cannot tell. Yet this dreadful traffic still goes on.

The action of civilized nations has, however, confined it to a single port (Macaow), and even there they are making some effort to "regulate" it.

The present traffic at Macaow consists of prisoners taken in the clan fights, which are of constant occurrence in the western districts of the Province of Quantung, and who are sold by their captors to Chinese or Portuguese man-buyers upon the interior waters, — of villagers or fishermen kidnapped along the coast by the lorchas still kept in the traders' employ, — and of Chinamen who, after having been enticed into the gambling-houses, sell themselves "as in honor bound" to pay their losses. There are established Coolie-brokers in the city who have a depot or private jail in which they put each Coolie as they get him until they have a full cargo, when they sell them "in bulk" to the highest bidder. They usually command a price varying from $ 10 to $ 27 per man, according to their physical strength.

During the years 1864 and 1865 there were nine thousand and seven hundred sold to Cuban traders at Macaow, and nearly three thousand at the port of Canton. How many were taken to that island as voluntary emigrants from other ports I could not ascertain from official sources. All these Coolies, voluntary and involuntary, are forced to sign a contract to labor for a term of years, and these agreements are sold at auction when the Coolies arrive in Cuba; usually bringing from $ 350 to $ 600, for eight years' service; during which time, and usually years after, the Coolie is entirely at the disposal of the purchaser.

It may be interesting to the reader to know what were the means adopted at the other ports for the prevention of this slave traffic, and below I give a condensed summary of the regulations at present in force at the port of Hongkong, from whence come nearly all the emigrants for America.

First. The harbor-master or commissioner shall by an interpreter question every Chinese emigrant to ascertain if he is going of his own free will.

Second. The name and occupation of every emigrating Chinaman shall be entered in the register, and sufficient time be given him between the registry and sailing of the vessel to visit his home and return.

Third. If the Coolie sees fit to remain at home he can do so by paying any advance-money that may have been given him and the cost of his food in port.

Fourth. No person under twenty-five years of age shall be allowed to emigrate without the consent of his parents or guardian.

Fifth. The ship-masters or agents must guarantee to the Coolie all his legal privileges in the land to which they take him, and shall pledge themselves to afford him the facilities for writing or of sending money to his friends.

Sixth. Persons detaining a Coolie against his will are subject to heavy fines.

Seventh. The captain of every vessel carrying Chinese passengers must make a detailed report to the authorities before he sails of the size of his ship, the accommodations for passengers, the quantity and kind of provisions he has on board, and the course he intends to take to reach his destination.

Eighth. Every such ship must have a surgeon and a sufficient supply of medicines.

Ninth. The owners or agents of the vessel shall be under bonds to deliver the Coolies at the port for which they are shipped, if not prevented by bad weather, accident, or sickness.

Under these regulations, which seem to be carefully observed, it is now a very difficult thing to carry away a Coolie without his consent. But his consent, as will be shown in a subsequent chapter, does not always indicate an entire free will in the matter.

The following table, which, owing to the lack of official records in some ports, and to the fact that vessels often take on large numbers from the shore after leaving the harbor, has been made up in part by careful estimates after an examination of all the official records that have been preserved, and will serve to give the reader some idea of the number of Chinamen taken away by force or fraud between the year 1847 and 1870. This does not include voluntary emigrants, nor any of the number taken to India, the Sandwich, or smaller Philippine Islands.

Having submitted these figures to a number of gentlemen who have had more or less to do with the Coolie trade, as some say they are too high and others too low, I venture to let them stand as they are. Several ship-loads are said to have left Shanghai and Foochow in 1853 and 1854, but finding nothing definite about them, I have omitted them from the table.

Destination.	Where Shipped.	From 1847 to 1850.	From 1850 to 1855.	From 1855 to 1860.	From 1860 to 1865.	From 1865 to 1870.
Cuba	Macaow	1,200	13,700	33,000	30,000	28,000
do.	Ports about Canton	1,000	17,000	2,000	4,000	1,000
Total	. . .	2,200	30,700	35,000	34,000	29,000
Java	Hongkong and Whampoa	. . .	2,000	2,500	. . .	. . .
do.	Canton	. . .	1,000	1,500	. . .	. . .
Total	. . .	. . .	3,000	4,000	. . .	. . .
Peru, the Chincha Islands, and other South American Colonies	Swatow	. . .	22,000	30,000	. . .	. . .
do.	Macaow	. . .	1,700	32,000	27,000	20,000
do.	Canton, Amoy, and Hongkong	3,000	7,000	9,000	18,000	2,000
do.	Whampoa and Cumsing-moon	. . .	13,000	13,000	. . .	. . .
Total	. . .	3,000	43,700	84,000	45,000	22,000
Indian Archipelago and Australia	Macaow and Ports about Canton	. . .	9,000	18,000	2,000	6,000

	Cuba.	Peru, &c.	Java.	Australia, &c.
Grand Total	130,900	197,000	7,000	35,000

It may be a matter of interest to the reader to know what has become of this immense number of unfortunate Chinamen. Statements, not very trustworthy however, have come to me from Havana, declaring that there were less than seventy-four thousand Coolies on that island January 1st, 1870. I cannot readily accept this account, because it does not seem possible that so large a proportion as one half have died since their arrival. Certain it is that few have ever escaped from the island, and if there are but seventy-four thousand left, the cholera, yellow fever, and the cruelty of their task-masters, have been more destructive the last five years than during the previous ten. In Peru and the adjacent islands the mortality has been much greater than in Cuba, owing to the unhealthy atmosphere of the guano islands, the total disregard of the Coolies' health by task-masters, and the enormous number of suicides. Some few have escaped from Peru and Chili by smuggling themselves on board ships bound for the Pacific coast of the United States, but the number is very small. In view of all this evidence, which would seem sufficient to condemn the world, I hold these nations engaged in the traffic to be guilty of *deliberate cruel, wholesale murder;* and feel as I shudder at their deeds, many too awful to be recorded by me, that an eternal "reward for the deeds done here in the body" would be eminently just and proper.

CHAPTER VII.

AMERICA AND CHINA.

Respect for America. — The Chinese Belief that the United States and China are to be united. — Settlement of Chinese in Mexico. — America known to the Chinese for Ages. — Marvellous Tales. — The Reports given by returning Emigrants. — The Action of the United States upon the "Coolie Trade." — The Missions of the Hon. Caleb Cushing, the Hon. William Reed, and the Hon. Anson Burlingame. — The Honors paid the latter. — American Literature in China.

THE great respect which the Chinese of all classes have shown for the American nation has long been a matter of surprise. Abused by drunken sailors attached to American ships, and often deceived by wily speculators claiming to be citizens of the United States, they nevertheless continue to reverence the flag and honor the nation. English travellers have noticed this fact, and accounted for it by saying that it was owing to our being so far away and so little known. One writer, who did not sign his name, stated in the "North China Herald" that he had found in the provinces of Honan and Hupee "a superstitious notion" that the American and Chinese nations were some time to be united, and says that one man declared that he saw in a vision "an immense bridge over to the United States." This "superstitious notion," taken by itself, seems almost too absurd to be repeated, and would not have been in this place but for some strange corroborative facts which have recently come to the writer's knowledge.

Ensign Charles Foster of the United States Navy, writing from Shanghai in June, 1857, states that, while they were discussing the propriety of joining with the English navy for the purpose of bringing the Chinese government to better terms, the vessel was visited by a native army officer. Upon being questioned about the indications of war and the idea that the American nation might take part, "He told his interpreter to say to us that the American and China nations are brothers. We could not fight China. The gods had commanded the shot of Chinamen to go over the 'Melicans,' and the shot of our guns would go harmlessly over Chinamen. He firmly believed that a war with America was impossible, on religious grounds." How they obtain these ideas has never been explained, nor to my knowledge has it ever been attempted; although for some years the fact of their predilections in favor of Americans has been universally acknowledged. I have no hope of establishing, beyond controversy, a reason for this feeling. But it is my intention simply to introduce the subject in order that other writers may follow it to its conclusion, and that any new facts coming to light which have a bearing upon the subject may be recorded and preserved by those who come after me. The following incidents may have some relation to the subject, and are given to the public for its careful consideration.

In a letter dated January 9, 1867, written by a Frenchman named Anthony Baillet, who seems to have been well acquainted with the social customs of the Chinese, and whose letter was sent to the Royal Society of Antiquarians, there is a rather remarkable statement, from which I venture to make an extract: —

"There is a curious tradition in which the present generation of Tingchauese scholars express the most implicit belief. I have heard it in several different localities and with but slight variation. It is in substance nearly as follows. There was a great family called Tooloong, which lived in the land of Fukien and became rich. When a great conqueror came from the North, and the Emperor Hia was not able to protect his children, Tooloong and his family joined themselves with some barbarian Jews (or Assyrian) from the West, and abandoned their homes in grief. They gave themselves into the hands of the Gods. The great Dragon watched over them by night, and Yu-wang-shangty by day. This poor family were hungry, and the Dragon brought them rice and garlic. They were thirsty, and Lwe-Koong sent them showers of wine. For more than a thousand days Tooloong wandered northward and eastward, until the icicles grew on the skirts of his garments; still the Dragon said 'Go on,' and Tooloong's heart was stout. Then they found a great bridge, as white as the summer cloud, and very strong. The barbarians hesitated, but Tooloong was brave. They all crossed over. On the other side was a new China, where no one lived. The trees were beautiful, and the beasts kind. Tooloong wondered. But they kept on till a land of flowers was seen in the distance. The barbarians said, 'Let us not go farther, it will burn us.' But Tooloong said, 'I stop not till the Dragon stop.' So they entered the land of flowers. Here they were blessed. The Gods were very kind. Tooloong wanted a pagoda, and one came up from a cabbage. He wished for a house, and great blocks of the stone mountain came and arranged themselves into a dwelling. Tooloong built great cities in the flower country, and died. Then some of his children tried to come back to China. But the great bridge was gone. So they all, with the exception of *Nung yang*, were sent back to the flower country by the Gods. He flew over on a cloud and told his kindred of the great things Tooloong had done."

M. Baillet states that "the Americans, whom the Chinese hear of as living in a great country to the North and East," are believed to be either the descendants of Tooloong, or in some way connected with them. Whether this tradition has anything but a local circulation among the people of Tingchau he does not state. But be it local or national, it is a remarkable tradition, when taken in connection with the great mystery that shades the early history of human life in this country. If it have any foundation in fact, it must be a reference to the manner in which America was first peopled. "The North and East" would very consistently refer to the direction of Behring's Straits. The bridge might have been ice, or an isthmus covered with snow, which has since been submerged, or simply a fabulous way of accounting for the passage about which little was known. The barbarian Jews may have been the "ten lost tribes of Israel," and the "flower country" a symbolic term for the land of Mexico. Then the "great pagoda" and the self-moving "blocks of stone" would consistently refer to those wonderful structures the ruins of which at Palenque and Uxmal astonish the antiquarian, and whose gigantic pillars, neatly carved decorations, and deep-hued frescos compare favorably with those of Egypt and Syria. It seems the more curious, as the tradition was found in the interior and not on the sea-shore. It is also a singular fact that the images of gods which are manufactured in the vicinity of the Bohea, or tea hills, near which Tingchau is situated, are the exact counterparts of the idols found in California, New Mexico, and Mexico, and to be seen in nearly every American museum. Another point is that the tradition was found in one of the two provinces from which come nearly all the emigrants for America. What influence it may have had upon the action of these emigrants, directly or indirectly, cannot now be determined. There are also books and essays written ages ago which describe America with singular accuracy under the name of Fusang.* It is said by Chinamen returning from California, that they find a race of people (Indians) in America who talk their language, which goes to corroborate the Chinaman's idea that America was first settled by their ancestors, and it cannot fail to influence their ideas of our country and people. How well their traditions agree with the evidences found upon this side will be seen at once by all who have given the subject any thought.

Another cause for the favor with which America is regarded among the lower classes, may be found in the superstitious stories about this country, circulated in connection with those touching

* "Yeuen, Kian Lui-han," Vol. XXXI.

the sad condition of the people at home, to which reference has already been made. Astrologers declare to the Coolie who comes to have his fortune told that the good stars are travelling eastward, and if he would prosper he must follow them. The alchemists have revelations telling them that the chemical for turning stones into gold is to be found in the United States. Tales of buried treasures on the Pacific shores of the New World, which can be discovered only by observing certain superstitious ceremonies, are circulated and told by nearly everybody in the vicinity of Canton. Some believe that certain of their guardian spirits have been seized with the "emigration fever," and have gone to California in search of gold. A few take the broad view that the Emperor, being the "son of heaven and the ruler of the world," his kingdom must include America; and as he holds possession of the spiritual, if not of the temporal powers, America, spiritually at least, must be governed by him. Wonderful stories, partly true and partly fabulous, are in constant circulation with regard to the Chinese in this country. Each returning Chinaman, like Marco Polo, favors these tales, by making doubly marvellous such incidents in his experience as would be sufficiently wonderful if told in truth and simplicity. As yet these superstitions are confined to the vicinity of the ports, and cannot by any means be said to be universal in all of them. But they are gaining ground every day, and who can tell what influence they may have when time, with increased excitement, shall carry them into the interior?

I was told by an enthusiastic admirer of the Chinese character, that when he asked a Chinese sailor on board of an American steamer what was the wisest saying of the greatest philosopher in the United States, he received in reply a perfectly accurate quotation from the Declaration of Independence, stating that "all men are created equal and are endowed by their Creator with certain inalienable rights; among which are life, liberty, and the pursuit of happiness." If he did receive such a striking reply, — of which I am free to say I entertain some doubt, — the sailor must have been a rare exception to the general rule. I do not believe, from what I have seen of them in California and in their own country, and from the testimony of men who have had the very best of opportunities for observation, that the great mass of returning Chinese have any correct idea of our system of government. Certain it is, that the rumors which they put in circulation about it are very far from the truth. It is also evident that these falsehoods have had a greater influence in accelerating emigration than the same number of truths would have had. Strange as it may appear, when we consider that the returners are usually men who can see but little gain by staying here, the exaggeration is almost always on the favorable side. Their report is snatched up by eager imaginative gossips, and by the time it gets a general circulation it has grown from a statement of men, money, and work, to be a fable of gods, luxury, and ease; forming a very different picture from the legends in circulation about local and governmental matters. Should the Coolie declare, upon his return from California, that he had been abused, cheated, robbed, and finally sent home penniless, nobody would believe him. His friends would accuse him of telling a falsehood to avoid making them presents, and the authorities would arrest him for trying to cheat the government out of its legal taxes. He had much better say that he has property, and try in some way to make his presents and pay his taxes, than to incur the disgrace and risk of a denial. All of which prevents the circulation of the truth, and increases the weight of the fabulous stories already believed.

Another most powerful reason for their faith in America is founded on the prompt action of our government officers in China in the suppression of the Coolie trade. When the lower provinces of China were wild with terror; and when fathers, brothers, sons, and daughters were being killed, maimed, or kidnapped by the traders, and the gods seemed to have given the poor laborers entirely into the hands of fiends and devils, the agents of the United States were the first to cry out against it, and practically the first that came to their relief. When the whole world beside seemed to be leagued for their destruction, and reckless adventurers from our own shores were found vile enough to deal in human misery, the consuls of this nation, for which they had ever entertained a profound respect, arose as a body to cry out against it; unfortunately for the Coolies and shamefully for the government at home, the United States took no special action as a law-maker, until 1862, when the following law was passed and subsequently enforced:—

"*First.* No citizen or citizens of the United States, or foreigner coming into or residing within the same, shall for himself or for any other person whatsoever, either as master, factor, owner, or otherwise, build, equip, load, or otherwise prepare any ship or vessel, or any steamship or steam vessel registered, enrolled, or licensed in the United States, or any port within the same, for the purpose of procuring from China, or from any port or place therein, or from any other port or place, the inhabitants or subjects of China known as "Coolies" to be transported to any foreign country, port, or place whatever, to be disposed of or sold, or transferred for any term of years, or for any time whatever, as servants or apprentices, or to be held to service or labor; and if any ship or vessel, steamship or steam vessel belonging in whole or in part to citizens of the United States, and registered, enrolled, or otherwise licensed as aforesaid, shall be employed for the said purposes, or in the "Coolie trade" so-called, or shall be caused to procure, or carry from China for the purpose of transporting or disposing of them as aforesaid, every such ship or vessel, steamship or steam vessel, her tackle, apparel, furniture, and other appurtenances, shall be forfeited to the United States, and shall be liable to be seized, prosecuted, and condemned in any of the circuit courts or district courts of the United States, for the district where the said ship or vessel, steamship or steam vessel, may be found, seized, or carried.

"*Second.* Every person who shall so build, fit out, equip, load, or otherwise prepare, or who shall send to sea or navigate as owner, master, factor, agent, or otherwise, any ship or vessel, steamship or steam vessel, belonging in whole or in part to citizens of the United States, or registered, enrolled, or licensed within the same, or at any port thereof, knowing or intending that the same shall be employed in that trade or business aforesaid, contrary to the true intent and meaning of this act, or in any wise aiding or abetting therein, shall be severally liable to be indicted therefor, and on conviction thereof shall be liable to a fine not exceeding two thousand dollars, and be imprisoned not exceeding one year.

"*Third.* If any citizen or citizens of the United States shall, contrary to the true intent and meaning of this act, take on board of any vessel, or receive or transport any such persons as are above described in this act, for the purpose of disposing of them as aforesaid, he or they shall be liable to be indicted therefor, and, on conviction thereof, shall be liable to a fine not exceeding two thousand dollars, and be imprisoned not exceeding one year.

"*Fourth.* Nothing in this act hereinbefore contained shall be deemed or construed to apply to or effect any free and voluntary emigration of any Chinese subject, or to any vessel carrying such person as passenger on board the same; *Provided, however,* That a permit or certificate shall be prepared and signed by the consul or consular agent of the United States, residing at the port from which such vessel may take her departure, containing the name of such person, and setting forth the fact of his voluntary emigration from such port or place, which certificate shall be given to the master of such vessel; but the same shall not be given until such consul or consular agent shall be first personally satisfied by evidence produced of the truth of the facts therein contained."

Connected with this action, in the Chinese mind, is the noble behavior of the Hon. Caleb Cushing, who, as minister from the United States to Pekin, in 1844, made a treaty with the Emperor, in which it was especially provided that the United States would not protect or encourage the terrible opium trade. In 1856 the United States sent the Hon. William Read as a peacemaker to mediate between China and the allied forces of the English and French, and in 1868 the treaty was made which recognizes China as being in every respect entitled to the same privileges as other nations, and offered the assistance of the United States, in all national enterprises tending toward a better civilization. This treaty has another merit, which to the Chinese mind is even greater than the text, viz.: *It was drawn and negotiated by the Hon. Anson Burlingame.* Whatever difference of opinion Europeans may have had upon the mission and statesmanship of that most noble representative of America, the Chinese looked upon him as a being almost perfect. Much to the honor of the man and the nation who sent him as its minister, their confidence was in no wise misplaced. By his generous interest in their history and literature, his straightforward manner, and admirable social and diplomatic qualities, he won their entire confidence, — something which no other foreigner has ever done. So great was their respect for him that, after his death while representing them at the Court of St. Petersburg, they gave him a tablet in the Temple at Peking, and prepared the way for subsequent deification. His life, treaty, and death has given the Chinese a confidence in our nation which, of itself, is sufficient to bring them unhesitatingly to our shores.

The literature of China, which is the pride of the higher classes, has received many popular additions from the libraries of America. Geographies, readers, philosophies, arithmetics, and grammars have been translated for the use of students, and novels, histories, and travels for general reading. But the most influential work ever rewritten from American authors is the Life of George Washington, as published by the Governor of Fukien a few years ago. It has had an extensive circulation in the provinces, and must go far toward giving a favorable opinion of the country of the "flowery flag."

American missionaries and hospitals have also done their share in the formation of public opinion, and counteracted in a measure the bad impression which the behavior of drunken sailors and early unscrupulous traders must have made. Other causes, one of which is mentioned in the next chapter, have been at work, and more are now being brought to bear, so that soon China will, as far as the Chinese belief is concerned, "virtually include America."

CHAPTER VIII.

THE NEW GOD, "WARD."

Sketch of Ward's early Life. — First Appearance as a "Filibuster." — His daring Deeds in Central America and Elsewhere. — His Appearance in China. — His disciplined Troops. — His Death. — Burial. — Deification.

IN an obscure town in the United States was reared a boy, who in his extreme youth was considered to be one of the brightest children of his class.* Later, however, bad associates and the loss of friends turned the current of his mind, and, instead of becoming an intellectual leader in all that was refined and good, he became a physical leader in all that was coarse and bad. With an unquenchable ambition for glory, and filled with the tales of heroes and adventurers, which unfortunately is the first kind of literature to which our youth are directed, he fought imaginary duels with the gods, and real ones with men, with a recklessness which was as odious as it was aston-

* Sketch of Ward's life by Yeuenkan.

ishing. As a farmer he neglected his crops, as a clerk he bullied the customers, as a sailor he was feared for his physical strength and hated for his overbearing disposition. He thought himself born to be a ruler among men. His unscrupulous ambition was his only god or guide. Hence, there was no adventure too hazardous for him if booty and praise were to be found in case of escape. In the proper channels of life his mind would have been a power almost irresistible. As it was, he either bore off whatever obstacle appeared in his path, or shrewdly cut his way around it, dodging about in his zigzag course to deal a blow or grant a favor. In fine, he was a generous, reckless dare-devil.

This man would appear in all sorts of places at most unexpected times. A street riot in New York, the deck of a man-of-war, a political meeting, or a church, is said to have been all the same to him. Such was his versatility of character and aimlessness of purpose, that it has caused him to be much misrepresented, many people thinking they knew and understood him well, when perhaps they had no acquaintance with his desires, or with many of his strange actions. Following to its natural sequence the bent of his uneasy disposition, he leagued with Walker in the wild undertaking of conquering the Nicaraguans and forcing upon them a democratic government which they did not want. In this connection he was first known as "Ward the Filibuster." His adventures in Central America in connection with Castellon's rebellion, his narrow escapes and deeds of valor, would fill an octavo volume of a thousand pages. For two years and a half * he was the terror of Grenada and Costa Rica, and if one half the tales of midnight attacks, secret expeditions, open battles, and murderous exploits which the people of Central America still circulate are true, he must have possessed almost supernatural powers of endurance and been wholly regardless of human life. True it is, that with his assistance Walker became dictator, and, but for the interference of the American and other governments, might have been at present the ruler of a flourishing empire. In May, 1857, the last of the filibusters left Nicaragua, and it was supposed that the disastrous result would deter them from any further undertaking of the kind. It is said that Ward went to San Domingo and to Cuba with the hope and expectation of inaugurating there a filibustering expedition of his own. However that may be, he gave the Pierce and Buchanan administrations much uneasiness lest he should embroil the United States in a war with the European powers. It is stated as characteristic of him, that he

* 1855 and 1856 – 57.

kept a copy of President Pierce's proclamation against filibustering * in his pocket and read it to his followers, saying that he wanted no one with him who would not fearlessly brave all the consequences. In 1858 he disappeared. After which there was an ominous silence in the filibustering world. So surprising was this quiet that the Boston Post, one of the wittiest of the American dailies, began an article with the words, "What are the Filibusters after now?" For two years little or nothing was heard of him, and his sudden disappearance was accounted for in various ways; some saying that he was in the slave-trade; others, that he was in the Mexican civil wars; while a third party circulated the story of his death "by a hundred bullets" in the Sandwich Islands. At last, in 1861, he was heard from, and, as might have been predicted, in an entirely unexpected quarter. He was in China, and filibustering still. Strange to say, however, instead of taking the democratic side of the question in China, which would have been more in spirit with his American education, he espoused the cause of the Emperor against the Ti-ping rebellion.

Lovers of Chinese history will remember that the Ti-ping rebellion was not only a revolt against Imperial tyranny, but also embodied a vigorous movement in favor of the Christian religion. At

* December 8, 1855.

the time Ward entered the service of the Emperor this rebellion had grown to such proportions and conducted its wars with such excellent system and such humanity, that a disinterested beholder would have declared the overthrow of the Imperial army to be inevitable. The scales hung tottering in the balance, with justice, law, education, and Christianity against cruelty, anarchy, ignorance, and idolatry, — the former being slightly in the ascendant. Christian men looked on with breathless interest at a struggle the result of which seemed likely to Christianize four hundred millions of people and bring freedom to at least two millions of slaves. The Ti-pings in their manifestos indorsed the Christian religion, abolished slavery, encouraged education, and cautioned their soldiers against the brutal or inhuman treatment of prisoners.* Their army included many of the greatest scholars of China. The territory they had conquered when Ward went to oppose them was the richest and best fortified part of the Empire.

The Emperor fearing the entire overthrow of his government, caught at anything which would be likely to help him in such an emergency, and most gladly accepted Ward's offer of assistance. Ward was the first foreign officer ever commissioned in the Chinese army. Immediately upon his entering into the compact he selected a body of five

* Lin Lees's "Ti-ping Revolution."

hundred Chinese and endeavored by them to introduce the discipline and tactics of European armies. As far as his own regiment was concerned he succeeded to such an extent as to make them almost irresistible in open battle, but no other branch of the army followed his example. This disciplined battalion under Ward's command, besieged cities, defeated armies, scaled high walls, made destructive raids, and one writer states that in two years they killed at least fifty thousand Tipings, or an average of one hundred to each man. Ward was obliged to lead, however, in every assault, and at Nanking had but twenty men at his back when he entered the city. Yet the rebellion grew. For every city that Ward captured the regular Imperial army lost at least two, and for every hundred men and women which his followers butchered a thousand came to take their places. The spirit of liberty was sweeping over the land and tyranny well might tremble. The people were rising to right the wrongs of two thousand years. The world was in sympathy with them, and the action of Ward called down curses on his head, and from no nationalities more emphaticaly than from the English and French. They even went so far as to set a price upon his head, and to send gunboats with detachments of soldiers under Admiral Hope to effect his capture. Soon there came a change. And such a change!

The Emperor feeling his helpless condition more deeply, since Ward's successes did not make his hold upon the government much stronger, sent to the English and French authorities special envoys asking for their assistance. With this request he stated, as a consideration, that he would open his ports to trade and would do all in his power to forward the financial interests of those countries. They accepted the proposition at once. The spirit of Mammon was abroad, and when did he ever fail to conquer? All sympathy with justice and Christianity fled at once before the money-god's magic wand, and the English and French fleets were instructed to attack the forts held by the Ti-pings and to co-operate with the Chinese army in the capture of cities. Ward, who the day before was a felon and an outlaw, was surprised with an offer of alliance from the same Admiral who had the day before been searching for him for the purpose of hanging him to the nearest tree, or shooting him in the presence of the army.* Soon he was offered a command under the English, and from that time forth he was the acknowledged ally of both France and England. Then came scenes of bloodshed that appalled the civilized world. Christian nations using all their power to stop the advance of civilization and the propagation of the religion of Jesus Christ! But Ward

* February, 1862.

never lived to see the end. In a little skirmish near the village of Tse-kie on the 21st day of September, 1862, he was hit by a Ti-ping bullet and mortally wounded. Three or four days after, at Ningpoo, this daring man closed his earthly career, after having requested a burial according to the Chinese customs.

Soon after his death his body, which had been placed in a beautiful sarcophagus, was taken to Soong-Kong, the scene of his earliest exploits, where it reposed for several years. In 1869 it was removed to the enclosure about the temple of Confucius, and a tablet in the temple itself erected to his honor, by order of the Imperial Government. Later it is said that he has been deified, and that the people are taught to respect America through the person of one of their own deities.

The deification of heroes is an especial prerogative of the Emperor, and every person receiving this honor becomes at once one of the gods of China. If the Emperor has received any especial service from an individual for which he has much reason to be grateful, he takes this way of showing his gratitude; *having always in view* the influence which it will have in binding more securely to him such persons as may desire to receive those honors for themselves. It is easy to see a deep and cunning purpose in thus raising an American to the dignity of a god. It serves to confirm in the minds of the people the idea that America is the friend of China and a strong supporter of the present rule. It sets an example before the people and indicates the reward that awaits such as die in his service. It creates a "God of Military Discipline," for the army to worship; the teachings of which will make its devotees more efficient. For these reasons, then, rather than the great service he was to the Emperor in putting back, perhaps for centuries, the civilization and Christianization of a great heathen people, Ward, the American filibuster, becomes ONE OF THE GODS OF CHINA.

DEPARTURE OF THE EMIGRANTS. — Page 211.

CHAPTER IX.

WHAT FOR.

Chinese going Home. — Why they left California. — And why they return. — What drove them from China. — Their Treatment in California. — Their Emigration voluntary. — Prospective Immigration.

EARLY one morning in the month of March, as I was standing on the forecastle of one of the finest steamers that has ever been built,* and looking with no little anxiety for the bluffs of the China coast near Foochow, which the captain had said we were nearing, a large company of Coolies came up from the steerage for the purpose of getting the first sight of land. It was to be the first glimpse of their native shore after a long absence in California, and I scrutinized them carefully. Imagining how I should feel if I had been absent from home the same length of time, and with what joy I should hail the first glimpse of America, I had expected to see in these simple-minded men demonstrations of delight, and per-

* Pacific Mail Steamship, 1870.

haps some strange exhibitions of what one writer has called "uncontrollable patriotism." But there was nothing of that kind. I thought that I saw tears in the eyes of one or two, when the great gloomy mountains first showed their outlines against the sky. And several smiled when, in answer to their inquiry, I said, "It is China." But cold, stoical, undemonstrative, the others listlessly walked the deck or sat themselves down by the wheel-house and indulged in a quiet chat. Nearer and nearer came the great cliffs, clearer became the atmosphere and brighter the light of dawning day, but the same careless look was on their faces and the same unconcerned air about their movements. Even when the junks in the bays and the cultivated spots on shore were near enough to see the Chinamen at work in them, these returners did not show in their faces any desire but that of idle curiosity. Some came up and glanced around the horizon very much as a farmer does in the morning when, querying in his mind about the probabilities of rain, he takes a moment's survey of the clouds from his door-step. They then went below to engage in a game of dominos, with a forfeit of twenty-five cents on each game. Some came so far up the gangway as to show their heads above the deck for a moment, and then turned back to take a pipe of opium in the steerage smoking-room. Yet they were going home! Going to the land of their birth, to their families, old acquaintances, old scenes, and old customs. "Have they no emotion? or have they such a command over their features and movements as to hide any feelings of pleasure they may have within? I will try and ascertain," thought I, and proceeded at once to question such as seemed in a talkative mood. The Chinamen are especially reticent upon their own affairs, and seldom mention anything in connection with themselves, unless pressed to do so. Fortunately I found two that were communicative, and to them I put the following questions, with the following replies in substance: —

Q. How long have you been in California?

A. Nearly eight years.

Q. Are you coming home to see your families now, or on business?

A. We come to see our families. But we do not know where we will find them. When we left them they were in a village near Canton, but we have not heard from them since we saw a man who emigrated from there five years ago.

Q. Do you expect to see them all alive?

A. We hope so. We have not heard of any raids or famines, and they were generally healthy. The police do not know that we are out of the country, and will not treat them harshly on our account.

Q. How do you hope to escape the law against leaving the country?

A. By going home quietly at night and keeping matters to ourselves.

Q. What would you do if discovered?

A. Just as we have done before. Pay the police and run away.

Q. Is it pleasant to go home under such circumstances?

A. No, it is not; and we shall go back again as soon as we can.

Q. Do all who return expect to go back to California again?

A. Not all. But nearly all.

Q. Why do you come home yourself, instead of sending for your family?

A. We must pay our debts, must provide for our aged parents, and know that our families do not suffer. The law will not let the wife come to us. Besides, if we could bribe them to let the family go, it would cost too much for insurance.

Q. What insurance?

A. Of a burial in China. It costs seven dollars per person.

Q. If you feel it such a duty to take care of your relatives, why did you leave China instead of attending to their wants at home?

A. Because *we could not stay at home.*

Q. Were you driven out of the country?

A. In *one* sense we were. The police kept arresting us for nothing we had done, the tax collectors took our rice and clothes, the landlords reduced our wages, and we were afraid the government was going to take us for soldiers.

Q. Do you love China?

A. Yes. But we mean to live and die in California.

Q. But are you not ill treated in California?

A. Yes, sometimes, *but not so badly as we were at home,* and we earn more money.

Afterwards I conversed with others on the steamer, and they nearly all said to me, as many others have said since then, that they left China "because they could not stay"; and liked California because they were treated better there than at home. They "could not stay" in China because the officers of government abused them, because they feared some calamity at home, and because their gods in a singular combination of circumstances said they must go, and spoke with a voice too stern to be disobeyed. They chose to come to America instead of going elsewhere, because it was the easiest of access, — their superstitions told them that here they could be happy, — and they had such confidence in this nation, owing to tradition and the deification of Americans, as to believe what was told them of the wages and wealth which they would find here. I do not think they came to find liberty, in its true sense, as they can have no idea what it is. They do not come to be citizens, or to enjoy the rights which they know the Americans possess. Not but that our duty to ourselves demands that they be treated justly, whether they expect it or not. Neither do they intend to adopt any of our customs nor any part of our religion. They do not intend to take any interest in the public affairs of the nation, though they should stay here for life. What they may think after being acted upon by the enlightening influences which circulate in this free atmosphere is another matter, and nothing to do with this book. As long as the present government of China is in power they will come here, if left to their free choice, in fast increasing numbers every year; and, although China is by no means crowded,* yet millions might come without being missed at home.† (God only knows what we should do with them all!) But a liberal change in the Chinese national affairs, by which the Coolie might enjoy the fruits of his labor, would — in spite of our gold — not only stop all emigration from China, but would call home every individual of them which adhered to the Boodist, Tauist, or Confucian religion. In fact, then, — at least as far as the Chinese are concerned, — America is truly what it professes to be, —

AN ASYLUM FOR THE OPPRESSED.

* See p. 30.

† The time has passed when persuasion is necessary to induce immigration, as is shown by the numbers crowding into the seaports of China awaiting an opportunity to obtain a passage.

HOW.

HOW.

CHAPTER X.

FIRST EMIGRATION.

The first Visit of Chinamen to California. — Slaves from Peru. — The first Chinese Miners. — No stolen Laborers landed.

THE popular idea that the first Chinamen who visited California were "gold-hunters" is now said to be a mistake. They came from Peru in two vessels that put in at Callao for repairs while *en route* from New York to San Francisco in 1848 or 1849. They were fugitives from their masters in Peru, and by pretending to have worked out their contracts secured employment as sailors; while others, by the assistance of these, stowed themselves away until the vessel was too far at sea to put them back on shore. There were about twenty of these men in all, and they were employed for some time at the rickety old wharf in San Francisco discharging the cargoes of sailing vessels which began to arrive at that port. One or two vessels from China with Chinese cooks and servants happening into port soon after, these wharf-men induced their countrymen to remain with them. In this way the number increased to a hundred or more, before they ventured out into the mining districts, — not one of which had ever heard of gold in California before their departure from China.

An old miner of my acquaintance once gave me a very graphic and homely description of the scene when the first company of Chinese made its appearance among the huts of the miners. He said that he was standing close beside the low door of his old bark hut, filling his pipe with tobacco, when he heard a succession of loud shouts and hoots "down toward the flats." He thought it might be that a party of Indians had come in, and the crowd of rough miners were enjoying themselves at the red-man's expense. The noise grew louder as it grew nearer, and everybody ran out of their cabins, some half dressed, some with frying-pans, others with kettles, which, as they contained the owner's dinner, could not be lost sight of, for fear of theft; and still others, with rifles and revolvers, ready for deadly encounter. He said that he snatched his old no-brimmed hat from the stake and joined in the general rush for the locality where the shouts and cries were loudest. From this point I will let him tell his own story. "The fellers hed made a rush to a spot behind an old Mexican cookin' ranch, and hed filled in all around it so tight that it was fifteen minutes before I cum to a view of the cause o' ther muss. Some of the chaps hollered, 'A ring! a ring!' and when they began to spread out, there in the middle, lookin' mighty skeered, was a lot o' fellers with long tails to their heads and short trousers, besides great broad-brimmed wooden hats and a pole like a neckyoke over each shoulder. They were queer-lookin' chicks, and no mistake. The chaps 'round made a big ring and yelled and hooted, an' finally begun to throw things at 'em to git 'em mad, but old Dick Losha stepped out in front o' 'em, and, with the revolvers in his hands, said, 'Look o' here, fellers, these ere chaps haint done no harm and don't know our talk, so yer see we don't want ter abuse 'em. They 've been sent up here to work, and there 's more a-comin'. We can hire 'em cheap when we want 'em, so let 'em stay; they 're better nor the cussed Injun anyhow.' All the fellers said, 'All right, old boy,' 'Let 'em come,' and sich things; so they went off, and I did n't see more on 'em for a week. The fellers hated 'em arter a while, though, an' I reckon they were mighty glad to leave for up Dutch Flat way."

It seems that the escaped Coolies from Peru, notwithstanding the temptation of gold, were more anxious to return to China and the families from which they had been stolen, than to stay in the mines, and they improved the first opportunity to get a passage home, either by work as sailors or the purchase of passage tickets. Their story of the gold-mines and of the freedom which they found in California induced many emigrants who were going in other directions to change their minds and come to America. Soon others returned home and repeated the tales, with many additions, inducing their friends, and all who heard the stories, to take measures at once for the pilgrimage to America. Glad news indeed for the afflicted poor of China! How they improved the opportunity will be the subject of the subsequent chapters.

I can find no confirmation of the rumor that ship-loads of stolen or purchased Coolies were landed at San Francisco in 1854. There may have been cargoes obtained by misrepresentation, and it would be hard to find a ship-load that has not some duped ones among the number; but no laborers were ever brought into San Francisco, as far as I can ascertain, who were either salable slaves in China or intended to be such after landing in California.

CHAPTER XI.

THE COOLIES' DWELLING.

Searching for the House. — The Stench. — The Hut. — The Description of the House. — The Dinner. — Tree God. — Wives. — Children. — Superstitions.

YOU will not find it on the highway! So don't try. It is the dwelling of the poor man we are looking for, not the owner of lands and slaves. Come along, then, and we will go down this narrow path toward the sea-shore. We will be sure to find one about here. These fields of garlic, cauliflower, and wheat, as well as the ruddy rice-beds we see stretched along the plain, are all the work of the Coolies' hands. Here in China we have two growing classes, — the rich and the poor, i. e. the official and literary, with the laboring and ignorant. The official has a whole block of houses for his residence, built around so as to enclose a square piece of ground for a garden, and he has a great many apartments in the building. Some for his wife, some for the boys, some for the girls, some for the slaves, some for the Coolies, some for visitors, and some for smoking, eating, sitting, and reading, with a spare one or two for beggars. He has furniture, too, — mattresses, chairs, mirrors, tables, dishes, &c. But the Coolie has no such mansion, no such rooms, and no such furniture.

You must look sharp or you will fail to see it here in this bamboo thicket. Stand on tiptoe! Do you see a large tree anywhere? "O yes, there is one. It looks like beech from this distance, but I presume that it is China oak." Let us go around this clump of bamboos and along the border of the rice-patch, toward that tree; for the laborers worship trees, thinking there is a spirit in them, and they like to build their dwellings near by one so that the tree-spirit will protect the family and building. Yes, there it is, just in front of the tree, by that little patch of wheat! Now we will see how he lives, so that we can tell it to our friends when we get back across the Pacific. Look out for the mud and be careful about the ditches. There! stop! don't you smell it? I do, and would turn back now if I were not obliged to go on. What a horrid stench it is, to be sure! I can't see how they live in it. Perhaps they get used to such things and do not mind them. Ho! There it is — the house — in plain sight now. That long hut with four doors. It is the dwelling of four families, each having one room. I wonder what they do with all those children when night comes? Twelve little cueless ones, three old enough to wear that awkward appendage, and the others in the field, probably. Take out your diary now and set down what I say, for reference, in case you should ever wish to write about it.

The houses are built of bamboo matting and of mortar. The matting is fastened to the poles which make the corner-posts, one sheet on the outside of the pole and another on the inside, leaving a space between the two sheets about four inches wide. This space has been filled in with mortar and beaten down so that when the matting decays there will be a hard cement wall left to support the roof. These walls or sides are about seven feet high. Have you got that written? Well; then say that the roof is of the old-fashioned "hip" style; two sides, running up to a ridge, and is made of bamboo poles covered with a thick thatch of wheat straw, the eaves of which project over the side walls about a foot. The door-ways are about two and a half feet wide, and are open from the roof to the ground. The door is a thick piece of matting, which is kept rolled up under the roof during the day and let down at night. There is but one window, and that is nothing more than a square hole cut through the back side of each room, with a groove-sliding board to close it in bad weather. Don't set this down as "a hovel" either, for it is one of the best Coolie dwellings in the district. Some are nothing but a tent of straw matting about four feet high. This you see has no chimney, for they never use fire inside, and have no floor, as you will see when we pass the door-way. Their door-yards are always like these, filthy and miry, and ever as thick with pigs and chickens. See that old hog, lying directly in the door-way of the second house. There comes the woman of the house. See! how she climbs over him, as though he had as much right there as she. I presume that he is treated better than she is by the master of the house. Notice the stagnant pools of dirty water all about, and that pile of rubbish in the edge of the thicket. No wonder we smelled the place when we were so far away. We will step in at this door and see what they have inside. Notice these door-posts; how they are pasted over with red paper, on which are curious Chinese characters; while here near the ground is a little niche in the wall about three inches square, with two joss-sticks burning in it. They burn so slow that you can see no smoke; but these little pieces will hold fire for many hours yet. That is the way this people worship their household gods, and keep away calamities. One would think that a little cleanliness would be better than joss-sticks for the latter purpose; but we must bear in mind that they are heathen, and do the best their education and circumstances permit.

Ho, ho! Nobody at home! They must all be out in the field at work, so we will walk in unbidden, and if the neighbors do not trouble us we will have the whole room to ourselves. Here! Let us drive these pigs and chickens out before we look any farther. There! now we can get along much better. Write now, that the only room in the Coolie's dwelling is but eight feet square, with the earth beaten down hard for a floor, and the rafters overhead for a ceiling. Little pieces of clothing are hung about on the bamboo walls interspersed with scraps of red paper pasted up as "tablets" to some spirit. Do you see that narrow shelf with that little comical image on it? See! How they have arranged the little bundles of luck-sticks, which look like bunches of toothpicks; and here are some more burning joss-sticks in this broken goblet. That is the god of the kitchen, and these little pieces of melon and ricecake near the joss-sticks is an offering to him. When the children come home and find that the little image does not want his dinner they will fall to and eat it themselves. He never wants it, and I suppose that they make calculations upon that when they place the dish before him. Here in this corner is a three-legged stool, and over there is a rough table about one foot wide and four feet long. Beside these, and a little bunch of straw near the door, there is nothing for comfort or convenience.

You don't see where they all sleep? Neither do I, unless they all wedge in together here on the dirty floor. Then no doubt they have the pigs and hens inside too, to keep those domestics from running away in the night or being stolen by the unscrupulous neighbors. Just think of it, eight persons, four pigs, and seven hens all sleeping together in a damp room eight feet square! Chinamen jabbering, babies crying, hens cackling, pigs grunting and squealing, — really, what a noise there must be when they wake!

Where are the cooking utensils? They must have a place somewhere for the purpose of cooking. Let us get out of this unhealthy place and go around to the backside. Here! Don't go that way! for if you do you will have all those dirty children after you. Why don't the parents wash their infants? Because the parents believe that in case they use too much water the god of that element will cut off their spiritual ears when they get in Hades, and pin their bodies to the wall of a fiery furnace for ten years. And, as they don't know how much water the god will allow them, they get along with just as little as possible. But here is the cooking apparatus — as I told you — at the backside of the house. Some of the family must be about here, for the fire is burning and the iron kettle is boiling most furiously. Now write down the description of a Coolie's kitchen. It is situated at the back of the house in the open air, and consists of a few brick laid up so as to keep the burning pieces of bamboo in place, while the cooking utensils consist of a kettle which sits directly on the fire, two sieves that fit in the top of the kettle one above the other, and a wooden bowl for a cover. Take off the cover and we will see what there is under it. Yes, that is vermicelli in the first sieve. Steaming is the best way to cook it anywhere. Lift up the sieve of vermicelli and see what is in the lower one. Ah, of course; that is rice! They steam that too. Lift up once more and see what is in the water beneath. Pork? So it is. Pork, rice, and vermicelli! This will make their dinner to-day, and I venture to say that the same material composes more than three hundred and fifty of the dinners of the year. When they come to dinner to-day they will take the sieves and set them here on the ground, and, after being seated all around, will slice the pork into the rice and vermicelli, and all eat out of the wooden bowl, using their fingers and those little chop-sticks, which look like pipe-stems, instead of knives and forks. Look! The other families have their dinners cooking in the same way. They never have any fire in the houses, and in cold weather try to keep themselves warm by putting on more clothing. They have very large and heavy cloaks made of braided straw, — all fringed on the outside, — which in winter gives them the appearance of being *thatched.*

Here is the tree we saw, and here the paper tablets pasted on the south side of it! See the joss-sticks around the roots, and the pieces of half-burned paper. It may have been two hundred years since the ancestors of these families began to worship the spirit in this tree; and, although they have suffered meantime for food and clothing, they have doubtless burned many a hundred dollars worth of paper "mock money" and joss-sticks to keep the good-will of this god. They very seldom let these sticks go out, and when the thunder god sends a rain, the poor people cover the sticks with pieces of clothing or matting to keep them dry and burning. These four families are all relatives and must join together in bearing the expense of this tree-worship, each paying his share.

Here come the children! what a disgusting set of little vagabonds they do appear to be! All dressed in frocks so much alike that you cannot tell the boys from the girls. Sore feet, sore eyes, sore hands, — poor little things! How I would like to souse you in the sea-water until you were clean, and having dressed you like children in America, exhibit you to your heathen father in a state of Christian tidiness and comfort. The hens and pigs are your companions, and, alas! seem to be the society in which you are the most fitted to appear. Where is your mother, my little man? See him run away from us as though he was afraid to have us take any notice of him; and there, all the others go after him. They don't understand our language, and think perhaps that we have come to steal them. We will walk around and see the mothers. Do you see that woman in a frock and long pantaloons, cutting bamboo-leaves for matting? She must be the wife of one of these Coolies. See that bag she has on her back, which makes her lean over as if it was heavy. That contains her little baby. If we should go out where she is, we would see its little head sticking out at the mouth of the bag and lopping back and forth as it tries to sleep as if its neck was out of joint. Sometimes it cries with the cramp, but the mother does not mind it, as she has to work hard to get enough to eat. When she gets an armful of bamboo-leaves, she will come back and see that the dinners are cooking as they should.

Here by this door-way is one of the grandmothers, seated on a stool and braiding the bamboo-leaves into coarse mats. It looks like the coarse basket-work we sometimes see in America. She will earn four or five cents to-day, if it is pleasant and she can sit out in the light. How gray her hair is! Notice her thick shoes, short dress, and strings of beads. She tells the fortunes and reads the signs of the family; and is almost a holy one in the eyes of the youth. They reverence their grandmothers more than they do any other member of the family.

Here is another one of the wives. Hear how she scolds at the children, and see how she has tried to powder and paint her rough face. Her hair as you will notice is combed straight back from her forehead and arranged in a curious waxed coil on the back of her head which resembles the ornamental handle of an old-fashioned pewter tea-pot. Her feet are not very small; for Coolies' children are seldom allowed to compress the feet and thus unfit themselves for the life of labor that must come. Women having the smallest feet cannot walk alone. This woman, you see, has very coarse clothes, homely features, rough hands, and big feet, yet she is foolish enough to think that she is handsome, and I have no doubt she was driving away those dirty children for fear that we would think they belonged to her. She is evidently as proud as she is poor. If so, her husband has met with a calamity in marrying her which all the gods of China cannot mitigate. See how proudly she stalks back into the hovel as we approach; for the purpose of showing us that she knows the airs of high life, where women are not to be seen by strangers. She had much better be attending to her husband's dinner, for which he will soon be leaving the rice-beds. But let us hurry and get away from this stench, which grows sensibly worse as the sun gets up, or we will have no appetite for the currie and rice that await us at the "Parson's," in Canton.

CHAPTER XII.

THE COOLIE'S RESOLVE.

Tales of America as told by returning Chinamen. — How an Americanized Coolie behaves. — Its Effect upon his Countrymen. — Emigration Circulars. — Central Pacific Railroad. — Copies of Advertisements, &c.

ANY returning adventurer who has been gone from his native village for several years feels that he must ponder upon the kind of a story which he will tell when his old associates — friends and enemies — gather about to hear of his exploits. The nearer he draws to the port the more important does this part of his duty appear to him. There will be many an anxious ear waiting for his story, and it behooves him, in view of the important position which he holds, to so prepare his tale that he may do his hearers and himself great credit. Even the pleasure-traveller, who takes only a short excursion to Europe, and who feels that he has seen nothing of the adventurous kind, will no sooner find himself comfortably housed on board a returning steamer,

SOLD FOR DEBT. — Page 224.

than his thoughts run quickly homeward to the loved ones, and as speedily return with the query, "What have you to tell us?" They seem to say, as each landless morning returns, "Prepare yourself, for the gown and slippers are ready, the ashes are brushed up around the hearth, and the chairs are all set for that magic circle to which you must tell your adventures." The traveller from China, Japan, and India, where marvellous things are said to happen, is in still greater perplexity with regard to the story he shall tell and the embellishments which it may need to make it interesting to children and old folks alike. So much of an object does it become to some men that they rush into all kinds of danger, endure serious hardships, and incur fabulous expenses for the satisfaction of having a "good story to tell" when they reach home again. Some few conjure up imaginary adventures, and try to tell them with the same spirit with which they would relate real ones; but these are even more expensive than the true ones, as they impoverish the moral and most valuable part of man's nature, and leave him no satisfaction when told. Better to risk his life on one that is real than to venture eternity on one that is false. This is the feeling among Christian and civilized men. How is it with the heathen?

Do the Chinamen after a long absence in foreign

countries feel any of the longings and responsibilities which we feel? Have they those sensations of anxiety in regard to the account which they will render of the time the gods have given them in America? I am satisfied that they have. Human nature is the same everywhere, subject only to the shades which circumstances give to it. The Chinaman in his childish pride must be even more anxious than are Europeans to tell to his credulous audience at home a thrilling and fascinating tale of adventures. But upon his imagination or invention are put none of the restraints of civilized Christianity, and no fears of a reckoning in eternity will disturb him in manufacturing a story of this kind. Given four solitary weeks of dreary sea life, when to possess something upon which to ponder is a coveted happiness, — with an uncertainty about the lawfulness of his return that keeps his home perpetually in his mind, the Coolie maps out his tales and lives over his California life with Aladdin-like additions. His hearers will expect something strange and wonderful, and it is far from his proud intention to give them any disappointment. Many times his tale is all he possesses when he reaches his home, and that usually grows in proportion as his cash becomes less. If he starts from San Francisco with a fortune in his pocket there is but little probability of his reaching home with it. I do not believe that, out of a thousand Coolies who return, more than two ever get to their destination with a *cash* in their pockets.

All the Coolies that have come to the United States, with only a very few individual exceptions, have come from what is called the "Canton District," and all of them upon their return are landed at Hongkong. If, in their gambling among themselves on board the ship, they have not lost their money, they are almost certain to do so in the hideous gambling-dens which the English government licenses in the Colony of Hongkong. Sharpers are always on the watch for them, and if they have never before had any inclination to gamble, their belief in chance as a dispensation of the gods will cause them to listen to the wily arguments of their Chinese tempters. Their arrival on the soil of China, and being so near home, together with the pretended friendships which suddenly seizes upon a set of native swindlers, and their own desire to show their wealth and importance, leads them into all kinds of extravagance, and gives to the thieves around them a most desirable chance to cheat or rob them of their money. If it should happen that they escape the claws of the Hongkong vultures, they will be pounced upon by the officials at Canton, or in the interior, under cover of the law against emigration, and fleeced of all they have, in the shape of bribes and fees, paid to escape the prison or headsman. If they should slip through the hands of one mandarin, by bribing him, that same official would send a courier ahead of the victims to tell the next mandarin of their coming, and how much money they have left. Notwithstanding these reverses, which are sure to greet the emigrant upon his return, and through which he is fortunate to escape with his personal liberty, he still rehearses his wonderful stories of the United States, for the exhibition which he has never for a moment abandoned. It has never been the writer's privilege to witness the return of one of these emigrants to his native neighborhood, but he has heard many an incident relating to the sensation which such an event naturally causes in the ignorant and gossiping Chinese communities.

The emigrant usually calls first on his aged mother or grandmother, to receive her congratulations, and then goes to the residence of his own family, if he is the fortunate possessor of a wife. Whatever changes may have occurred in his religious opinions while in America, he usually returns ostensibly a more devoted idolater than when he went away, and his first thought, after being restored to his wife, is of an offering to the gods in honor of his return. This is performed by the Boodist priests, and the whole family, including such friends as he chooses to invite, join in the ceremony. This celebration serves to spread the news of his coming; provided the ready mouth of gossip has not already made the "wanderers return" well known to all that ever were acquainted with him. After this, if he keeps clear of the officials, he will be called upon by old and young, hailed by the urchins in the streets, and be a kind of living prodigy among all classes. He will receive invitations to every feast, where the lower classes are admitted, and will be made the especial subject of sacrifice on the next regular day for temple-worship. He is naturally willing to believe that the people's ideas of his nobleness is by no means false; and, in the enjoyment of his temporary glory, does everything he can to show his greatness. He walks as they walk in California, holds his head as they do in San Francisco, talks down in his throat like the miners, and acts in many respects as some foolish American women do just upon their return from the foppish city of Paris. He talks about "muchee dollar," and "me catchee pidgeon," with all the dignity of a San Francisco banker. He slides his skull-cap over on one side of his head, gloats in high boots and a shirt collar, and otherwise astonishes his less-favored associates. He rehearses his prepared tales to the wondering multitude with a pompousness that astonishes even himself. He tells of great mountains of gold, where all a man can lift is had for the taking. He gives it as his opinion that a piece of gold the size of a thumb-nail is worth ten thousand million of *cash*. He says that the Chinese gods rule in California and give to him whatever he asks for. He goes into particulars; and devotes an hour to the description of the big blue, black, and white devils he has seen in America, and the great battles he has witnessed between them and the gods. The joss in San Francisco is said to talk with men and rebuke the barbarians who come in to abuse him. He says that the Celestial inhabitants of the Pacific Coast are applauded by Americans for their parentage, and feared because of the great Kingdom from which they came. He himself has been offered the superintendence of a mining country where there were millions of people and any number of great palaces. Wine and all kinds of food to be had for the asking, and little or no work. He has been head comprador of a princely establishment where he had a thousand American servants.

Soon, he begins to tell larger stories, and continues to increase the size of his tales until they are too much even for the heathen, and by "overleaping himself" falls to the ground. There is much more danger lurking around the person that is too popular than threatens the man that is too much hated. And I am told that the emigrant, after a few weeks of vainglory, is glad to escape the ridicule that begins to be thrown at him by such as would hail his downfall with envious joy.

Whatever may be the *ultimatum* of the emigrant's experience as an exponent of Chinese life in California, his stories do have an astonishing effect upon his old acquaintances. They may ridicule and sneer, yet they feel convinced that there is something in the fables which they have heard. They contrast the emigrant's haughty bearing as compared with that he wore when he left them, and, seeing that he has better clothes now than he could formerly afford, they form an opinion at least favorable to America. The poor Coolie goes to his hard, uncomfortable hut, after hearing of the free California, with a discontented feeling. He grows uneasy as he resumes his accustomed task, and thinks of the happy life in the United States about which he has heard. He has a vague idea that he would like to go and see for himself. Weeks pass, and he hears of gifts for the gods from Chinamen in California, and of presents to a family from their friends across the Pacific. Tales of rich Chinamen in the United States begin to multiply, and under their influence the Coolie's discontentment gradually and steadily increases. He chafes under restraint, gets disgusted with his family, despises his work, hates his landlord, quarrels with the tax-collector, and makes himself and everybody about him generally miserable.

No such fables were ever introduced or credited about any other country. Nearly all the Coolies for the colonies of East India go from the open ports of China, where they have had more or less contact with foreigners, and know exactly what they are going to do when they arrive at their destined habitation. The proximity to China also takes away a great deal of the romantic and marvellous, while with those who have frequent intercourse the affairs of the colonies are an every-day matter of fact. None but skilled workmen are wanted or accepted, and consequently but very few of the very lowest classes ever find their way there.

Not so with the United States. To these ports *everybody* is encouraged to go, and much better inducements are held out to the Coolie or laborer than to the skilled workman. The idea the most dwelt upon by emigration agents is that the United States is glad enough to get anybody, and that the ignorant or partially educated Coolie is just as welcome and as likely to obtain employment as are the merchants or higher classes. "Equality" is the most potent doctrine used to induce them to go.

These ideas the Coolie turns in his mind from day to day, not daring to mention his thoughts to any one lest he should be considered as an offender against the laws and suffer accordingly. The idea suggests itself, perhaps, that he is plotting something unlawful, and it would not be surprising should his conscience, if he has any, upbraid him and make him the more uncomfortable. Just at this time, perhaps, comes a circular sent out by some ship-owners or contractors through the Chinese brokers, informing him that a vessel is taking Chinese passengers for California or New Orleans. It also states, among other inducements, that the laborers shall have $ 30 a month after their arrival in America, and a comfortable passage across the Pacific Ocean. These circulars are always couched in language easily understood, so that if a man can read at all he can easily master the contents. Everything is explained as far as can be, including the value of $ 30, and the cost of a ticket, in Chinese currency. Suggestions are also made about the most speedy way of disposing of property and getting into Hongkong, from which port all American-bound emigrant vessels take their departure. A copy of a circular issued in the Chinese language, and sent into the country around Canton by a Chinese broker's establishment in Hongkong, was translated for me, from which I make the following extract: —

"Americans a very rich people. They want the Chinamen to come and will make him very welcome. There you will have great pay, large houses, and food and clothing of the finest description. You can write to your friends or send them money at any time, and we will be responsible for the safe delivery. It is a nice country, without mandarins or soldiers. All alike; big man no larger than little man. There are a great many Chinamen there now, and it will not be a strange country. China god is there, and the agents of this house. Never fear, and you will be lucky. Come to Hongkong, or to the sign of this house in Canton, and we will instruct you. Money is in great plenty and to spare in America. Such as wish to have wages and labor guaranteed can obtain the surety by application at this office."

No sooner does the discontented Coolie read this, if he is able to decipher it, or hear it read, if he cannot, than he feels that the time for the move which he has contemplated has come. Here is a chance for the poor man to escape tyranny and want and become independent and happy. His forefathers have said that America was a happy land, and he has heard that a Chinese family first settled on its flowery domain, and now the gods seem to point to it as a way for him out of his trouble. Who knows what thoughts fill his brain and quicken his heart as he lies down upon the cold damp ground of his hovel the night after the receipt of the circular, *resolved to emigrate to America!*

While the agricultural Coolie is making his

resolve there are thousands of others who arrive at the same conclusion at nearly the same time. Circulars and runners often misrepresent the condition of the Chinaman in America, and, for the purpose of filling a ready vessel or making out a contract within the stipulated time, give reasons for their haste which are not sustained by the truth. They offer to the laborer, whether he be a weaver, carver, tailor, hatter, or farmer, a lucrative situation in America where he will be employed at his own trade. They say nothing about the cost of living in the United States, and leave it to be inferred that it will be no more expensive than it is in China, while the wages will be twenty times as much. They even go farther, and most grossly misrepresent the accommodations on board the ship, the food that will be furnished them, and the reception they will be likely to meet when they arrive in America; as will be seen by the appended copies.

Although brokers and other interested parties have been in the habit of publishing circulars upon the subject whenever a cargo of Coolies was wanted, yet the first occasion, as I am told, on which they met with any definite return was at the time of the great demand for laborers to build the Central Pacific Railroad. The construction and equipment of that road was one of the most important projects ever undertaken, when considered in a national point of view. Some men are foolish enough to believe that America owes its present unity as much to the construction of that track as to the armies under General Grant. However that may be, it was very necessary to the government and to civilization that the road should be completed at the earliest possible moment. All that the constructors asked for from the national council was granted without hesitation. Money and acres were given away by the million and much treasure squandered that would have been saved by a little delay. But no! California was in the balance, and nothing but some great enterprise undertaken in her behalf by the national law-makers would keep her men and gold in the Union. The Pacific Road was that enterprise. How gigantic it seemed, and with what wonderful speed it traversed the deserts and encircled the mountains is well known; and the astonished nations of the earth have not yet ceased to wonder. At that time the isolated State of California was not sufficiently supplied with laborers to carry on its own liberal enterprises, and consequently was ill prepared to undertake the grading of a thousand miles of railroad, which must mount to the snows, descend to the blooming valley, and bore through rocky ridges, again and again before it reached the great basin of Salt Lake. In this exigency an appeal was made to the Chinamen. "Come over and help us!" echoed across the Pacific. "We have money to spend, but no one to earn it," said the despatches to Hongkong.

Then the brokers began to print their circulars, the boarding-house keepers to rearrange their rooms for temporary lodgers, while the authorities entered upon fresh expedients for preventing anything but free emigration. Meanwhile couriers scoured the country from Swatow to Liuchau, and from Yangkiang to Nanngan, scattering the invitations everywhere and proclaiming to the wonder-struck Coolies that a great nation had need of them. These couriers went into the hovel and told of fine houses, into the rice-swamps and spoke of healthier occupations, into the workshops and ridiculed the pay, and lost no opportunity, so long as the officials left them free, to sow discontent in the already desponding hearts of every laborer's family. Men who had heard of America only as a land of fable, where none but the good were allowed to go, heard it then for the first time in connection with themselves.

They came. Every valley and mountain in Fukien, every plain and river in Kwantung, contributed to the army of labor which was to give to the Union peace and prosperity. So many came to the ports that there were not ships enough to take them; and years passed before all had left Hongkong who came there to answer the invitation sent by the Pacific Railroad. Since that call there has been but little difficulty in obtaining ship-loads at any time for America. For the result of the investigation of the subject at that time, corroborated by such as have returned, gave the people who heard of it great confidence in America and its people. So much has this continent eclipsed the countries of Asia and the islands of the Pacific, that it is with the greatest difficulty laborers can be found for any but North American ports. Ships have been in Hongkong harbor for weeks, and the owners have spent large sums of money in advertising for Coolies to be taken to the Sandwich Islands, without getting a dozen men. Yet all the Chinese boarding establishments were in the mean time filled with Coolies waiting for the departure of the Pacific Mail Company's steamer for San Francisco. This "emigration fever" steadily increases, and it may be safely estimated, that, from this time forth, if no measures are taken to prevent it, the number of Coolies coming to this country during any one year will be doubled during the subsequent year.

Translated copy of a circular issued in 1862 *by a comprador in Hongkong, who contracted to load an Oregon vessel with emigrants.*

"TO THE COUNTRYMEN OF ARR CHEAU! There are laborers wanted in the land of Oregon, in the

United States, in America. There is much inducement to go to this new country, as they have many great works there which are not in our own country. They will supply good houses and plenty of food. They will pay you $ 28 a month after your arrival, and treat you considerately when you arrive. There is no fear of slavery. All is nice. The ship is now going and will take all who can pay their passage. The money required is $ 54. Persons having property can have it sold for them by my correspondents, or borrow money of me upon security. I cannot take security on your children or your wife. Come to me in Hongkong, and I will care for you until you start. The ship is substantial and convenient.

(Signed) "ARR CHEAU."

Another circular, issued in 1868, read as follows: —

"GREAT PAY. Such as would be rich and favored by *Shan*, come to the writer for a ticket to America. The particulars will be told on arrival.

(Signed) "SHOO MING."

One issued in April, 1870, contains the following most extraordinary statements: —

"All Chinamen make much money in New Orleans, if they work. Chinamen have become richer than mandarins there. Pay, first year, $ 300, but afterwards made more than double. One can do as he likes in that country. Nobody better nor get more pay than does he. Nice rice, vegetables, and wheat, all very cheap. Three years there will make poor workmen very rich, and he can come home at any time. On the ships that go there passengers will find nice rooms and very fine food. They can play all sorts of games and have no work. Everything nice to make man happy. It is nice country. Better than this. No sickness there and no danger of death. Come ! go at once. You cannot afford to wait. Don't heed any wife's counsel or the threats of enemies. Be Chinamen, but go."

Several other translations of these advertisements have been put in my hands by friends, some of which state the plain truth, and contain trustworthy information upon the manner of conducting business in America. But the larger part of them use the most extravagant and, in some instances, outrageously false expressions, and can be excused only on the plea that exaggeration is the habit of Asiatics, and that whatever is said or written is understood to be true only to a certain extent. I am sure, however, that many people reading the statements that there was "no sickness in America," believed it and acted upon it when nothing else could have moved them.

CHAPTER XIII.

CONSULTING THE GODS.

Expectations. — Obligations to Boodah. — Inquiries of the Kitchen God. — Dreaming on the Sea-shore. — Methods of Consulting the Deities. — Spiritualism in China. — The Interview with a Medium. — Farewell Ceremony by the Priests. — Preparing the Spirits of Ancestors for the long Absence of the Coolie in America.

WHEN we left the Coolie in the last chapter he had just made up his mind to emigrate.

How he was to reach Canton or get from that city to the rendezvous in Hongkong was, perhaps, a perplexing enigma. If he felt as other races feel on the eve of such important events, he must have passed the night in restless tossings, building and rebuilding air-castles of the most chimerical material. He would think of his family and what they would do without him. He would imagine how pleased his children would be and how proud it would make himself, to come back with a princely fortune and astonish his old neighbors. Then the harrowing thought returns of his present poverty, and the doubt there is of his being able to pay his fare to San Francisco. He feels that he must go, to escape the awful suffering in the shape of mental and physical toil which he is daily enduring, because there is no hope in rebellion. His children will be like him in circumstance and prospect, unless he does some such bold thing to relieve them. He *must* go. But how?

After exhausting his own expedients, and finding nothing feasible, he turns to the supernatural, as man is apt to do, and determines to make inquiry of the spirit-world. He has been educated to believe that communications can be carried on with the spirits in heaven or hell, if the questioner will only comply with certain conditions, and that it is a meritorious action to make such inquiry in times of distress. He feels that the subject is of sufficient importance to be taken before the image of Boodah, which sits in a little tile-covered shed that stands on a hill several miles away, and is called a "temple." If he had the time to go there, and the money to lay out in offerings, he would cast lots in the presence of the god to get the answers he requires. But as he has neither of the requisites for obtaining the evidence of the greatest god, he must be satisfied to take up with a lesser divinity; just as the idolatry in some Christian churches gives to the rich man the highest seat with a waste of religion, while in the back pews by the "gloomy corner" there are men and women suffering for the crumbs which the rich man spoils. For it is a state of society bordering on idolatry, where the rich man, in the eyes of men, is a fitter candidate than his poor neighbor for the honors of eternal life. The Coolie, in his poverty, feels this privation, and, *believing* that he has no such opportunity as the wealthy official to secure a happy hereafter, adds it to the long list of grievances which he has already made out against his China home. Thrown upon the lesser spirits for the replies that Boodah should give, he determines to inquire first of the kitchen god, which chubby image even the poorest hovel in China could not be without. So, in the absence of room to perform his ceremonies in the overcrowded hut where his family are sleeping, he arises noiselessly from his hard cot, and, taking the little image and his straw cloak, steps out with them into the damp and starlit night.

Over the ditch into the rice-fields goes the poor devotee of a false religion, carrying in his hand the image or being which he considers to be possessed of divine power and wisdom. Strange, strange infatuation! Soon he emerges from the mucky swamp, covered to his knees with the black mud of the paddy-field, and walks hastily down to the sea-beach. Here he will find a roomy bed for himself and a rocky pedestal for the image.

He has made up his mind to *dream* out the answers to his unsolved problems, and will ask the god to guide his visions. He places the god carefully upon a sand-covered stone, in an upright position, and in accordance with his local superstition, takes all the *cash* he has in his pocket and places them in little piles of sevens on the sand before the idol. Then, retiring a little way he swings his clenched hands up and down, and, making three low bows, falls upon his knees. Then placing his forehead on the ground he makes many promises to the god; among which are money and rice, when he returns from California. To bind the bargain he begs the deity to take the *cash* already offered. In consideration of all this, he pleads for a dream, the interpretation of which will show him some way to get a passage to San Francisco. Then rising to his feet and looking about to assure himself that no one sees him, he wraps his coat of thatch about him and lies down upon the sand to dream. The dull, eternity-like ocean comes with its crystal, life-like bubbles, and laughingly breaks them on the beach below, while the thirsty freedom-seeker looks up at the stars, and longs, and listens, and sleeps, and dreams.

If, when the morning breaks and he takes his way with the image back to the hovel, he has had any dream of a certain road or of certain men he will be safe in concluding that the god had answered his petition. In which case he would be very likely to take advantage of the suggestion at once. But if his dreams were fitful, unconnected and hard to remember, as, in his disturbed state of mind, would most likely be the case, he will make up his mind that he has taken the wrong method to obtain an answer. For the sake of continuing the subject we will suppose that the state of his mind is in accord with the latter proposition, and follow him to the next ceremony which his superstition requires him to perform.

If he has sufficient time before the beginning of his hour of work to consult the god in other ways he will drive the family out of the hovel, and after replacing the god on its accustomed shelf and returning the cash to his pocket, will take a short piece of bamboo-rod and drive it into the floor or prop it in an upright position with bricks or blocks of wood. From the top of this short piece of rod to some object on the other side of the cabin he will stretch a stout piece of cord, taking care that it is slightly at an angle with the shelf on which the idol sits. Having done this he selects a small chip of wood and balances it on the cord about half-way between the rod and the other fixture. Having gone thus far with his preparations, he presents his petition by repeating it three times, and prostrating himself for a few moments before the image; always being careful to so word his request that it can be answered by yes or no. He then takes a stick, and, striking against the upright rod beneath the string, causes the latter to give a sudden jerk throwing the chip into the air. If the chip falls on the side of the string next to the Coolie, his petition is answered in the affirmative; if it falls upon the other side, the answer is in the negative. The Coolie's first question would naturally be, "Is it best for me to go to America?" The chip falling on his side shows the reply of the god to be "Yes." "Shall I get much money?" "Yes." "Would it be well for me to go now?" "No." "This year?" "No." "Next year?" "No." Here is a dilemma, and the Coolie goes back to ask the first question over again. This time he gets "no" for an answer and immediately suspends the ceremony, as a "yes" and a "no" answer to the same question are supposed to show the idol's unwillingness to answer any more queries. This not only stops inquiry by the "string method," but by all others; and the Coolie, who, but for such a result would have questioned further — by tossing up a piece of money with heads for "yes" and tails for "no," or by drawing at random a numbered stick out of a bunch, the number of which refers to some of the classified sayings of the sages on the affairs of life, — is now forbidden further consultation. These having failed, through the obstinacy of the god, in this case, the Coolie must seek other sources of information if he would go to the golden land of America.

I wonder if the spiritualists of this day in New England ever think that their belief is "nothing new" either in theory or practice; or that it has been known and believed in China for more than twenty-three hundred years? Not only do the Chinese spiritualists believe in the same agencies and the same results which distinguishes the sect here; but they also practice all the methods adopted in this country for spiritual communication, and a hundred others that do not seem to be known here. By this means they determine what their deceased relatives are doing, — how they live and what they eat, — what are the troubles and pains of purgatory and what is the remedy. They believe that the land of purgatory is like this earth socially and politically, with the exception of the absence of work and wages. The spirits are supposed to eat, drink, sleep, quarrel, fight, sing, dance, &c., just as they did on earth. But as life is as expensive there as here they can have but little joy unless the relatives on earth send them money enough to pay their expenses. During the stay of the spirits in that nether world, which is but temporary, they are possessed of certain powers, by means of which the gods expect them to make their wants known to men. They can rap on chairs and tables, and move the kitchen furniture with the permission of the kitchen god; they can make noises in the air, play on musical instruments, show their footprints in the mud or sand, sprinkle water on the face of the dead, pull the hair or clothes of the living, take possession of human beings, and after putting them into a trance, talking through them; and, in a thousand other strange ways, show their presence and desires. The most common method pursued by the Chinese is that of the medium, or "talking with the human mouth"; and to such a source will the Coolie go for the information which the kitchen god has refused to give. With a few cash in his pocket to make the medium a present he hurries to the hut of a neighbor whose wife, son, or daughter is possessed of the articulatory organs which the spirits like to use in their communications with men. Among the wealthier classes, he would not be permitted to see, and much less to communicate with, a woman belonging to another family, no matter whether the spirits took a liking to her or not; but he and his neighbors are too poor to stand on points of etiquette in matters where the other world is concerned. So he visits the female medium in the hut by the sea-shore with perfect impunity, and with little regard for etiquette makes known his wants together with the present he has brought. The medium is a girl

CHINESE SCHOOL ON THE AMERICAN PLAN. — Page 245.

about eighteen years old, who wears short hair, a man's hat, bone rings on her ankles, and otherwise distinguishes herself by strange decorations and wild manners.

At once upon his making his request, and giving her a piece of paper on which is scrawled the name of the ancestor whose spirit he wishes to invoke, she seats herself upon a stool in the centre of the room, and, closing her eyes, waits patiently for the appearance of the spirit. It sometimes happens that the spirit called for is too busy with some affairs of his own to be drawn away by the ordinary means, in which case he sends another spirit in his stead. The applicant is sure to get a communication from some one, and in cases where the spirit called for has left Hades to take up his abode in the body of another man or in some beast, one of the "seven" come to speak for him. These "seven" are the jailers or overseers in Hades, and have entire control of the souls of deceased men, and when one has so conducted himself there as to gain their good will, they permit him to go back to the earth again, in the shape of a wolf, bear, buffalo, or child. They ever after hold him in kind remembrance, and are always accommodating when any of his relatives have questions to ask of them concerning worldly gain. All spirits, however, make the same impression upon the medium when they begin to take possession of her body. Their presence is indicated by various starts and nervous twitches, with an apparent inclination to sleep. When these symptoms appear, the Coolie prostrates himself before the medium with his face to the ground and waits with anxious suspense for the awful words which the spirit uses at the beginning of her communications. With a series of mumblings and exclamations, which the devotee supposes to be something wonderful because they are unintelligible, the medium lifts up her head, shakes herself, and with closed eyes announces her readiness to answer any questions that the Coolie sees fit to ask. At this point he lifts his head and seats himself "tailor fashion" on the ground. Then putting the palm of one hand on top of his head begins his inquiries: —

"Is this the spirit of my ancestor?"

"Yes."

"Do you know what I come here for?"

"Yes."

"Will you tell me how I can get to America?"

"With money."

"How am I to get any money?"

"Borrow it."

"Who will lend it to me?"

"Anybody."

"What security can I give?"

"Your wife and family."

"Who will take that security?"

"You will find it if you search."

"Who will I ask?"

"The elders of the next village."

"When must I start?"

"At once."

"Will I come back very rich?"

"Yes; richer than a mandarin."

"Will my family be safe and will they continue the worship of my ancestors?"

"Yes."

"Will they all live till I come back?"

"Yes."

"Is America such a nice country as the printed paper said?"

"O yes. It abounds in every luxury and is free from pain and sickness."

"Are all my ancestors willing that I should go to America?"

"Yes; but you must send them large sums of money before you start, and keep them supplied afterwards."

"Must I go to the priests and ask them to appease Boodah?"

"Yes."

"Will my family be willing that I should go to America?"

"Yes, if you tell them that I, their great ancestor, advise it. Have you any further questions?"

"No."

Here the Coolie prostrates himself again, while, after various sighs and twitchings, the medium opens her eyes and declares that the spirit has gone and she will take the *cash.*

The light-hearted Coolie, fully satisfied that he will find a way out of his perplexities and return from California wealthy enough to be free, hastens back to his hut to tell his family.

One would suppose, judging by the exhibitions of human nature in our own land, that his wife and children, together with all the other near relatives, would be much grieved at the idea of parting with their friend and protector. If they are so, they do not show it. The wife — a slave to husband and employer — has no word of discouragement when her husband has decided to go, and is too superstitious to interpose her will against that of the deified ancestors. Some of the children may cry, if they have not reached that age where cruelty and privation prune away the buds of human affection. The wife trembles at the idea of becoming security for a debt which accident or inclination might so easily make her responsible for; but she is too well trained in the harness of servitude and too faithful a believer in spiritualism to interpose the slightest objection.

Having thus arranged all things to his satisfaction, and having not the least doubt but that, when he asks the elders of the adjoining village, they will fulfil the promise of the spirits, he proceeds at once to prepare his relatives in the other world for his long absence. They must have money with which to buy spiritual food and clothing, and his family will, in his absence, be too poor to supply them, until after money has been received from him. So he prepares enough to keep the spirits with strict economy until he has time to reach the United States, earn money and send it home. This spiritual money is prepared in many ways. The Rev. Justus Doolittle speaks of tinfoil and certain kinds of paper as being used for this money at Foochow, and the Rev. Dr. Albau at Teinsin, of pieces of skins and scraps of bark used for the same purpose. In Fukien, this money is made of almost any available material which can be marked with ink, — paper, bark, bamboo-leaves, tinfoil, cloth, and various other things having been seen in use. The Coolie, who has no money to purchase expensive material, will strip the dry leaves from the bamboo-bushes near his dwelling, and, with the assistance of the family, will cut them into little square blocks and cover them with writing, or with strange marks which look to him like letters. Little garments are also cut out and marked for the purpose of supplying the spirits with clothing. Each piece is prepared with such care that the manufacture is really a very slow process. It will take him and his

family many spare hours to make a sufficient supply to last the spirits during the nine months or more which it will take for a return of money from America. But when it is finished, and, by a consultation with the kitchen god, he learns that the spirits will be satisfied with the amount, he encloses small bunches in little paper boxes prepared for the purpose, and marks upon the cover the ancestor's name for whom it is intended. One of these boxes is placed before each ancestral tablet, — which is usually a piece of paper pasted up with the ancestor's name upon it, — and there burned to ashes, while the Coolie prays the ancestor to accept his "meagre gift." Some of this money is also burned for the benefit of the kitchen god; and the tree at the back of the house comes in for its share. Food, in the shape of rice-cakes and vegetables, is then offered to the gods and to the ancestors by setting it apart from the food of the family for a short time, joss-sticks are lighted in various places, and the ignorant Coolie supposes that his ancestors are provided for.

One more duty remains to be performed before the Coolie has completed his superstitious tasks, which consists in a sacrifice to the "three greatest gods." This is done to obtain the personal good-will of those divinities as well as to secure their protection in case the Coolie should be threatened with the vengeance of any of the ten thousand

other gods with which his imagination peoples the heavens and the earth. This is to be a sacrifice which will cover all the other offerings that his poverty obliges him to omit. I am not able to decide whether these "three greatest gods" are the three forms of Boodah, or the "pure ones" spoken of in published works on the Tauist faith; neither do the laboring classes understand the distinction between them. This ceremony is often performed, however, among them in the interior townships of Quantung when any great undertaking is to be inaugurated. The Coolie collects all his available cash, and going to one of the "work priests" who dresses, lives, and labors like the common people, makes as close a bargain as he can for the ceremony required. This priest associates with himself two others of the same class, or, as has been stated, gets one of the gowned and shaven priests from an adjoining temple or monastery, and proceeds with them to the house of the Coolie. Before their arrival everything has been cleared out of the little square room, and the whole place, outside and in, swept with the greatest care. The family all put on new clothes, if they have any, and wash the old ones if they have not, and the children even go so far as to wash their faces. A quantity of tempting rice and vegetables is prepared and the neighbors invited, so that the ceremony will be imposing and the dinner well attended. All the hopes which the family have of future prosperity, and all their native pride, is centred in this ceremony, and they spare no pains in making it as genteel and interesting as possible to both gods and men. It begins with the appearance of the priests, who are met a little way from the dwelling by the Coolie and his oldest son, who kneel before these officials and in that position receive their blessing. Then the father leads the way to the house while his son follows behind the priests; and upon their arrival, the whole company about the door-way bow nearly to the ground and remain in that position until the priests have passed in. The Coolie and his family then kneel about the threshold with the invited guests, and continue in that position during the performance of the idolatrous rites. The priests unroll a large sheet of paper, upon which is painted the figures of three men seated side by side, supposed to be the "three great gods," and fasten it to the wall of the room near the window. Underneath it they place the narrow table, and arrange upon it a row of wax-candles and a bundle of joss-sticks. After repeating a verse from some religious writer, and bowing toward each other, they pass several times around the room bearing a gong, a bell, and a wooden box, upon which they tap in slow and measured beats. Whenever they pass before the picture of the idols they make a low bow and rap their foreheads, reminding the European looker-on of Catholic worship. The candles are afterwards lighted with great ceremony, and the march around the room resumed, while the priests keep time to the beats of their gongs, with a medley of strange words, supposed to have much influence with the "three great gods." This continues for a half-hour, after which the gongs, etc. are laid aside and the candles carried around and around, — the priests lifting them up and pulling them down with a jerk, on each emphatic note in their meaningless chant. When the ceremony has lasted an hour or more, the priests ignite the joss-sticks, and then, with more chant and much more gong music, the good-will of the gods is supposed to be gained. Now comes the request for protection. Small round rice-cakes, cups of vegetables, and heads of wheat are set before the pictures, and after a chant and a prayer the priests leave the hut for a few moments, to give the gods time, if they should wish it, to partake of the dinner unobserved. On returning they declare that the gods are not hungry, and will be much more likely to answer the Coolie's petition than if they had been hungry and ill-natured. They then take a fresh bundle of joss-sticks, and, setting them before the gods without lighting, take away the burning ones and extinguish them. These partly burned, sticks are then carefully mixed with a fresh bunch, and, after being tied, are presented to the Coolie with instructions to draw one. The ends which are shown to the Coolie are those which have not been charred, while the blackened ends are concealed in the hands of the priest. If he draws a fresh one, the reply is in the negative ; but should he select one that has been charred, the reply is in the affirmative.

Sometimes the priests choose to let the Coolie ask his own questions while the joss-sticks burn. If so, they give him two pieces of wood which look like a round wooden ball sawed into two equal pieces. These he puts together, and after a chant, lets them fall to the floor. If the round sides come down, the gods will not notice his case. If both round sides come up, he has received "No" for his answer. If one round side and one flat side comes up, he has received an affirmative answer to his petition. The reception of this reply closes the religious ceremony. The priests then tie up their gongs, bells, etc., roll up the picture of the "three great gods," put out the candles and joss-sticks, and join the waiting company gathered around the dinner-kettle at the back of the house. The sons of the Coolie assist him in setting out the trays of rice, wheat, and vegetables, while he extends a pressing invitation to all present, and offers a meek apology for a dinner which he knows to be one of the best. Each guest comes supplied with chop-sticks; and, with many good wishes for the Coolie's safe return, they show by their present action how well they will enjoy another dinner when he shall be rich enough to invite the whole township.

CHAPTER XIV.

THE LOAN.

The old "Contract System." — How the Chinese were deceived. — The Action of the United States Congress. — Pledging Wife and Children for a Ticket to America. — The Coolie's Thoughts on leaving Home. — Village Elders and their Election. — How they assist the Emigrant. — The Mandarin's Fee. — Swindling a poor Man. — Signing the Bond.

IN order to understand the reasons which lead the Coolie to his next step, we will divert the attention of the reader for a moment with a reference to the "Contract System," which, so far as North America is concerned, the law of the United States has destroyed. When the moral and legal power of all the civilized nations, with the exception of Spain and Portugal, was brought to bear against the "Coolie Trade," it did not put an end to the heinous traffic, as all noble-minded men expected, but only served to restrict it to certain ports, and to cause its promoters to adopt a new name for the same crime. They called it the "Contract System." Through this nomen they sought to convey to the world the impression that the Chinamen whom they carried away were persons who had entered into contracts to pay their passage-money after arriving at their destination. These contracts bound the Coolie to pay so much per month, or to work a certain length of time, as a consideration for his passage across the water. But as the duped Coolies could not read the contracts, and usually signed the papers before the blanks were filled out, it left the ship-owners, or the planters to whom they transferred the contracts, with no restrictions whatever. In cases where the fare for the passage was only fifty dollars, the laborer was made, without his knowledge, to sign a contract for eight or ten years' work. The fact that the vessels would not receive a Coolie who wished to pay his fare in advance is sufficient evidence of their evil intentions. The gentleman whose generous statesmanship prompted him in framing the United States Law upon the "Coolie Trade" doubtless had these facts in view when he so worded it as to forbid the use of American vessels in the transportation of Coolies under the contract system. By it* a heavy fine as well as a term of imprisonment was imposed upon every individual who voluntarily aided in procuring or transporting such laborers. None but voluntary emigrants were allowed in

* See page 103.

American vessels, or in foreign vessels bound to American ports. No Chinaman would be considered a voluntary emigrant unless he paid his fare *in advance*, and was unbound by any contract to labor after his arrival in the destined port. This law is in force still.* At the time it was passed it may not have been thought how much

* Congress, in 1864, passed an "Act to Encourage Emigration," which created the office of Emigration Commissioner, and made valid contracts with emigrants in foreign countries in the following language: "All contracts that shall be made by emigrants to the United States in foreign countries in conformity to regulations that may be established by the said Commissioner, whereby emigrants shall pledge the wages of their labor for a term not exceeding twelve months, to repay the expenses of their emigration, shall be held to be valid in law, and may be enforced in the courts of the United States or of the several States and Territories; and such advances, if so stipulated in the contract, and the contract be recorded in the recorder's office in the county where the emigrant shall settle, shall operate as a lien upon any land thereafter acquired by the emigrant, whether under the Homestead Law when the title is consummated, or on any property otherwise acquired, until liquidated by the emigrant; but nothing herein contained shall be deemed to authorize any contract contravening the Constitution of the United States, or creating in any way the relation of slavery or servitude." This law has never been applied to Chinese emigration by the commissioner, and would be of no avail if he attempted to do so, as the Chinaman seldom acquires any property upon which the contract would be a lien, and the only security the lender of money could have, *as he has no control over the movements of the borrower*, would be simply *the word* of the Coolie, which for many reasons no European business man would take in such circumstances.

it would affect our own country, or what its consequences might be in China. The traffic with Cuba and the islands of South America was at that time the exciting theme, and was made of greater consequence just then by the complaints of other nations, who declared that the greater part of that terrible trade was done in American ships. Its only effect upon the trade with Cuba and South America was a transfer of the lucrative traffic from American vessels to the ships of other countries. But its effect upon emigration to this country was great indeed. Before that, a Coolie who had no money or available property with which to pay his passage could make a contract, either with the man in California who needed his services, or with a native "Society" or brokerage establishment in that State, by which he would receive his ticket, or the money with which to pay for it, in advance. In that way he contracted to pay only the face value of the ticket, and was sure that in a country like the United States no Cuban system of swindling or enslaving would be countenanced or permitted. In a land where, according to the rules of its fundamental law, all contracts must show "a consideration," or, upon application, be declared null and void, there is little danger of an overcharge for a passage-ticket, or of an underration in the value of the laborer's wages while paying for it. This the Chinaman is shrewd enough to understand, and he would gladly enter into contracts to be fulfilled in the United States when nothing could tempt him to make the same bargain to be carried out in India, Spain or Portugal. But this law cuts off all negotiation with regard to the payment in this country of debts contracted in China; so that, for the last eight years, the Coolie has had no choice but to pay his fare in advance. If he cannot do this, no ship-master would run the risk of taking him on board.

Out of the large number that left Hongkong in the year 1869 for the United States, nearly one third belonged to that class of coolies who own no property and who can scarcely live from day to day in China on their wages. The others belonged to the next higher class, who may be the owners of cabins, pieces of land, or other property sufficient to secure a passage, and yet be far from the danger of want or even of starvation in case of any accident. Among the higher or partially educated classes money can be borrowed of friends with or without security, so that if a man is poor himself, his wealthier relatives may advance him the necessary funds. Of this class few ever emigrate; as they consider themselves well situated in China. Of the very highest classes, none ever go out of their native country. The lower classes are consequently the only persons affected by the United States law, or who would be benefited by any change. They are the most anxious to emigrate, and yet must undergo the greatest hardships to get out of the country. Being a little better than slaves, they do have a few recognized rights, and among these is the right to sell themselves or their families. This property right in one's family is recognized by all classes, although in some localities no free person can be sold into slavery by parents without his or her consent.

Chinese slavery is said to be less irksome than was African slavery in America. Yet, as the buyer has an exclusive and entire ownership, and as human nature in China has the same coarse features that it has in other countries, I venture the opinion that slaves in some localities in China see hardships that the African seldom or never saw in America. Chinese slavery is not, however, strictly hereditary, and when a Coolie sells his son or daughter, he is not supposed to convey any right to the services of his unborn great-grandchildren. This right to sell also includes the right to mortgage; and the Coolie who has no other goods or chattels to offer as security in the payment of his passage across the Pacific Ocean, may pledge the life-services of his daughter, his son, his wife, or of the entire family.

Understanding thus much of Chinese custom we will follow the Coolie in his search for money. He has been told, as it will be remembered, that by an application to the elders of the next village he will ascertain how he can procure a ticket for the United States. This advice, however, was wholly unnecessary, as the first thing which the Coolie himself would think of doing would be consulting with the elders. To these petty officers go all the lower classes in cases of trial or perplexity, and as these men are elected to office by a vote of the freeholders, they usually listen gravely to every petition, with an eye perhaps to a future vote. In fact, they are the only officials to whom the laborers can apply. Every other officer in the nation is appointed and removed by the Emperor; and, apparently for fear that his officials may loose their dignity or make local connections which would be dangerous to the government, the Emperor seldom keeps them in one locality over three years, and does not permit their wives or children to live in the same town with them during their official term. Such appointees, like military post commanders in civilized countries, have no interest in the locality, and care too little for the people and too much for their own personal comfort, to be pestered by the ordinary grievances of their subjects. Nothing of a private nature would receive their slightest attention, unless a fee in the hand, or prospective, was shown as a retainer. The Coolie knows full well that he is attempting to break a national law while making an effort to leave the country, and hence he is circumspect and wary. He knows also, as every one must know, that the law in China is not supposed by any of its executors to apply to such violators as have the cash with which to make a bribe. He therefore provides himself (not always honestly we fear) with a liberal fee, and with a bamboo neck-pole and baskets, — the former for the elders and the latter to deceive the police, — and starts across the rice-plats, over the creek, and around the grave-covered hill toward the village, where, to his narrow mind, is concentrated all the wisdom of the known world.

If we were inclined so to do, we might stop awhile to speculate upon the Coolie's thoughts as he trudges along intent upon the great undertaking which he has before him. Tyranny, superstition, and fear of unexplained and flexible laws may have stunted his higher moral and intellectual faculties, and developed the baser part of his nature ; yet man in the lowest state is susceptible of some emotion when about to part with familiar scenes and faces. The Coolie may not be an exception. He does not own the cabin he is leaving, and he has nothing about it which he may truly call his own. So much trouble with so little of civilized refinement may have made his family a burden to him instead of a joy. Nevertheless, he has formed attachments for the locality in which he has always lived, that he will not feel until the act of parting strains and breaks them. He is conscious of these strange emotions this day, perhaps for the first time in his life.

He looks back at the cabin where his mother and his children can still be seen gazing after him, and wonders how he will feel when, in America, the mornings come and go, with no wife to prepare his meals, no children to hail his coming, no aged parents to give him counsel, and no old neighbors with whom to play at dice, or to gossip away the stolen hours. He looks at the rice-fields, notices the ditches he has dug, the furrows which he has so often trod, and the growing weeds that he has so many times destroyed; and he tries to realize at present what his feelings must be when he shall see them no more, and questions whether they will wear the same appearance when he is away. He sees before him a hundred graves upon the hillside, among which are those of his ancestors. The broken earthen pots which once held the bones of men, with their contents, lie scattered and neglected, the joss-sticks before the still unbroken receptacles have been wet by the rain or broken by the wind, and the fire, like the love which lighted them, has long gone out. The graves of such as have not yet been exhumed for lack of earthen pots to store their bones, or because no recent death in the same family had made their removal necessary, are overgrown with weeds, fern, and brier-vines. Sacrilegious hands have broken the pots, and ruthless feet have trodden the graves, yet the locality is none the less dear to him. His superstition and religion teach him that the ground is sacred. The mysterious influence of *Fung Shuy* has imparted such miraculous power to the soil that the burial of an ancestor beneath its surface guarantees prosperity to his descendants. There he hopes to be carried when his soul, goes down the dark road which leads to Hades. He believes that unless his body shall at his death lie within the limits of that cemetery, his soul, homeless and foodless, and perhaps headless, will wander a beggar and an outcast through the by-ways and slums of an eternal purgatory. Such are the teachings of his superstition, and believing in them as sincerely as he does in the existence of Boodah, he trembles at the thought of a possible burial in a foreign land. It may be that he thinks the voice of the brook is sweeter on this eventful day than it has ever been before. It is possible, too, that the trees seem greener, the rice-drills more attractive than they were before he entertained a thought of leaving them. And, who knows but that he often pauses in that short journey and consults with himself whether it would not be better to turn back at once and abandon forever the idea of emigration? He experiences, perhaps, the sensation of dread which we sometimes feel when we undertake enterprises of a dangerous and uncertain character; undecided whether it were not better to

> "bear those ills we have,
> Than fly to others that we know not of."

But when he recalls his years of labor, the wages for which were long ago spent in procuring the necessaries of life, and remembers the insulting words of the landlord, — the damp walls of the prison-house into which he was thrust by the tax-collector, — how one of his children was sold to pay a debt and how another died for lack of medicine or acceptable gifts for religious sacrifice, — how he has toiled for land, yet owns not a foot, — how secret spies are dodging his steps to arrest him for breaking laws the existence of which is still a matter of doubt with him, — how the graves of his family have been desecrated and the bones carried away by the law-breaking followers of some moneyed enemy, he no longer hesitates. For all this the gods now seem to have provided a remedy. In America he can earn, according to the terms in the circular, thirty dollars per month, which will soon make him rich enough to buy the cabin that he has so long occupied and the adjoining rice-plats, as well as to repair and decorate the family graves.

This, with a round sum laid secretly by for the purpose of bribing the officers of law and justice, as becomes a Chinese gentleman, is all that he asks or expects. By means of these possessions he and his family may reach the summit of human happiness. Who could hesitate long with such darkness behind him and such brightness ahead !

The dignitary toward whose office the inquiring Coolie directs his steps has been called by previous writers "the elder," although there is little analogy between the church or civil elders of civilized communities and these officials. Chinese elders, as the native word seems to signify, are but little more than superintendents of police and municipal judges combined, — "local fathers," whose duty it is to chastise the evil-doers and settle such quarrels as are not of sufficient magnitude to affect the affairs of state. These "local fathers" are elected by the people of the village to which they belong, and are supposed to represent the popular choice. They are the only officers not appointed by the Emperor, and their term may be long or short, — for a year or for life, — according to the vote of the people at their election. At first thought, one would suppose that this right of electing their own municipal officers was a redeeming feature in the government, and one which would be likely to prevent crime and official extortion. But in those provinces whose inhabitants have many representatives in the United States this right of election is nothing but the "present of a halter with which to hang themselves." Having this voice in the municipal affairs, the imperial officers expect good order and firm loyalty from all the people, and where they do not find it they hold *all* the people of the locality responsible and punish them all alike. If one man steals, the whole village is often fined. If one murders and escapes, the whole village must suffer a fine. The principle is, that the people have the power to prevent crime, and if they do not the Emperor will call them to account.

In China, as in every other country, there are always two or more parties at each election, but, unlike the parties existing in democratic governments, they usually bear each other a deadly grudge. The bad execution of the laws leads the people to organize in their own defence, and when a member of a family is accused of a misdemeanor, all the relatives try to save the honor of the house, by a united effort to get him acquitted. Of course the friends of the injured party are equally anxious that he should be condemned. This leads to hostilities between the friends of the accused and the accuser, in which the other citizens of the village usually take part, exercising, however, a choice of sides. Soon the whole community joins in the *mêlée*, and the two clans often temporarily settle their difficulties by mobs, street fights, grave robbing, and other acts of lawlessness. Nearly every village has its two principal clans, between which there is perpetual war; and these include numerous clannish subdivisions which circumstances make of importance or otherwise. The war between the principal clans is carried into the municipal elections, and the clan having the largest number of adherents is sure of carrying the election, and of placing men in office as "elders" who will clear the innocent and the guilty alike of the dominant party and condemn every person whom they accuse. When this is accomplished it behooves the defeated partisans to "change the color of their politics" and join the successful party, or they run the great risk of losing their property and of being sold into slavery or to Coolie traders, through the connivance and villany of the opposite party. On the extermination of one party another arises within the fold of the successful one, cutting it into contending factions whose difficulties will not be healed until another election or a bloody street fight shall place one greatly in the ascendant. Thus an "elder," instead of being an upright judge and a careful superintendent of the police, is simply the leader of a faction. His police are all selected from the most rabid of his electors, and as, like nearly all the petty officers of justice in the Empire, these officials work without pay, and depend upon their plunder and the bribes they get in concealing crime for their support, one can imagine how far this right of election tends toward public peace or domestic happiness. It makes petty tyrants of the elders, and if they happen to be agreed upon a general plan of conduct they will hold great sway over the cowardly people. In any event, they will be feared if not respected. To such an individual does the Coolie apply for instruction.

At the entrance to the elder's office, which is usually in some narrow, dirty street, the Coolie meets a number of policemen. They look in his empty baskets, scrutinize his dress, ask him his name, and what he is there for, and otherwise annoy the rustic with their impertinence and officiousness. In the entrance-way where he leaves his baskets he finds servants or sentinels who follow or precede him until he is almost lost in the crowd which hurries him on toward the "awful presence." At the door of the apartment, used by the elder as an office, he is told to enter by a policeman whose business it is to guard the person of the elder, and who stands eying the Coolie from the door-way during the entire interview. The Coolie's first business is to produce his cash and say that he wishes for some information, which the spirit of his ancestors, through a medium, had told him that the elder possessed. The sight of the cash, together with the compliment which the ancestor has seen fit to pay the elder, can scarcely fail to make him good-natured and accommodating, and he declares in the politest terms his readiness to serve the Coolie to the fullest extent of his power. The Coolie then makes known his errand, by speaking of his poverty and the prospect there is of riches in America, and asks the elder to show him a way to procure a ticket. The elder of course knows all about it. He has had many cases before, and some of them he has since learned have gotten rich. Has the Coolie a family? and if so, has he any robust, healthy girls, or well-behaved, industrious sons of a salable age? The Coolie thinks that he has. Well, then it can easily be arranged. Give security on them and borrow the money. But who has the money to lend? The brokers in Hongkong of course. But how is the Coolie to reach them? O, the elder will arrange all that, and will get the ticket for the Coolie just as soon as he can draw up and execute a bond on the Coolie's family. The Coolie is overjoyed. How much will a ticket cost? The elder cannot tell until he gets it. There will be *some cost besides the price of the ticket,* but it will make little or no difference to the Coolie, who can earn *so much* when he gets to America. When the time for the execution of the bond has been fixed for some day in the subsequent week, and the grateful Coolie has expressed his thanks, the elder escorts him out by the sentinel with a word of caution about expressing his intentions in the presence of government officials. Once by the disagreeable policemen in the entrance-way, the Coolie shoulders his baskets, and with a light heart goes singing and smiling back over the hills, to the old cabin by the rice-beds, feeling that the fates, spirits, and gods are now for the first time all on his side.

The elder doubtless smiles too. If he does not, his abstinence cannot be attributed to the lack of a good reason for so doing! He has not only received a good fee and placed it securely in his strong box, but there is a fee in prospect to which the one received is but the veriest pygmy. I have no doubt that the august elder deemed the poor Coolie's prayer for assistance of so much importance that he straightway left culprits in prison waiting for the dispensation of his justice, and even refused to hear cases in which prominent members of his own clan were interested, in order to attend to the procuration of the Coolie's ticket. His first business is with the mandarin. For, in an undertaking where even an obsolete law is to be violated it is well to know how the higher officials will interpret the action, and, besides, the elder has neither money nor credit to loan the Coolie for so long a time; while it may be that the mandarin has. Possibly the mandarin's office is in the same village, or at least in the next one, and thither repairs the petty official, feeling as much trepidation at the idea of entering into the audience-room of the mandarin as did the Coolie when visiting him. But the prospective fee finally urges him to the necessary steps, and he soon finds himself in the "hall of justice," confronted by the surly manchu mandarin. To this personage the elder tells his story, and requests the assistance of the mandarin in procuring the ticket, at the same time suggesting that they could charge an advance on the original price, and the mandarin should have the larger share.

O most potent fee! How like a tyrant thou enterest into cottage, hall, or palace, saying unto the inmates "Do thou," and they unhesitatingly obey. Like that many-formed god of Grecian fable, you change your shape upon every new occasion! But whether in the form of friendly gifts, servants' hand-money, Arabian "backsheesh," Coolies' "cumshaw," or mandarin's "squeeze," your power is still the same. Men swear falsely in your presence that never falsified before. Judges see innocence through an adamant wall of guilt, legislators change their views upon matters of public interest, nations forget their obligations to humanity upon thy slightest bidding. Hearts harden and melt, riches come and go, and the understanding clears, or thickens, at the merest indication of thy will! He that has thy good-will is possessed of a greater power in the world of reality than was imparted by Aladdin's lamp in the land of fable!

The mandarin's face lights up at the idea of the prospective fees, and with a cordiality that astonishes even the avaricious elder the mandarin accepts the proposition, and thanks him for submitting the case so generously. Then, with smiles and bows, good wishes, and renewed invitations to call again in similar circumstances, the elder leaves to the mandarin the work of carrying on the scheme for assisting a Coolie to break the law of China.

Straightway a swift-footed messenger leaves the office of the mandarin, armed with a bundle of papers, and under instructions to proceed at his liveliest pace to the distant city of Canton. He is a government messenger, recognized by his dress and gait; and toll-gates open, ferryboats hasten, pedestrians give him room, and sedan-chairs turn out, that he may be able to give his important despatches into the hands of the ticket-broker in Canton. This in due time is faithfully done, for a fee has been promised him upon his return. The broker finds in the bundle of papers an order for a ticket to San Francisco, for which the mandarin promises to pay, with a high rate of interest, in one year. There being no better security than a mandarin's word, the ticket, or the broker's promise to give it upon the application of the Coolie, is properly made out and given to the messenger, while the mandarin's letter is carefully filed away and marked "payable one year from date, forty dollars, with broker's fee, ten dollars and interest." Upon the return of the messenger, the mandarin adds fifty per cent to the fifty dollars which he is now bound to pay the broker, and sends a note for "seventy-five dollars* with interest payable ten months from date," asking the signature of the elder. To this note the elder signs his name, and shortly after receives the broker's ticket.

The next transaction is by bond, and a lawyer must be called to draft one. These semi-learned pettifoggers are as plenty in China as in America, and are as prompt to respond to the call of a fee. Therefore it requires but a short time to write a bond, by means of which the Coolie acknowledges an indebtedness to the elder of one hundred dollars with interest, and to secure the payment of which he pledges the persons of his wife, his three sons, and his two daughters. If he should fail to pay the amount in nine months from date, either at the Chinese banking-house named in San Francisco, or at the office of the mortgagee,

* I speak of *dollars*, as to estimate it in *cash* would only puzzle the American reader.

then the family may be sold forthwith; together, if they will bring money enough to cancel the debt, and singly, if no one person can be found to buy them all at a reasonable price. This done, the Coolie is sent for. He has no knowledge of the first cost of the ticket, and if he expresses astonishment, upon his arrival, that the price is so high, he is told that with thirty dollars a month in America he can pay it in less than half the time named in the bond. Unhesitatingly he then signs his name, or instructs another person to do so, takes the ticket, and, scarcely dreaming that a failure of payment is possible, returns as gayly as before to his family to rejoice with them in the delightful prospect which the possession of that ticket gives them all, and to prepare for his long and perilous journey.

CHAPTER XV.

PACKING UP.

Preparing to leave Home. — Assistance by the Neighbors. — An amusing Incident. — What the Family think the Laborer needs in America. — The Perplexities arising from too many Assistants. — Going to the Seaports in Wheelbarrows with Sails.

ONE would suppose that very little preparation is necessary where a poverty-stricken Coolie like the one we follow is about to start upon a journey. Nevertheless, there is nearly as much work attending his departure as there is employed in moving a whole civilized family, household goods and all. I witnessed some of these ceremonials at a Coolie's cabin on the Island of Victoria, and the bustle, fuss, and gabble made such an impression on my mind that I always involuntarily call up that scene whenever any reference is made to the subject of Chinese emigration. The Coolie was endeavoring to arrange his personal effects and at the same time to take leave of friends, so that both duties should be accomplished before the departure of the Pacific Mail steamer at noon. Little boxes of wood and paper lay about the door, while the only spare suit of clothes which the Coolie possessed was hanging on a pole near the cabin dripping with the water of a recent wash. The bamboo shoulder-pole, with the two baskets pendant, was balanced over the end of an upright stick near the door-step, while the load which the Coolie and his friends were piling into them was divided into parts of equal weight so as to preserve the equilibrium. There were at least twenty persons, including his wife and children, hard at work about the cabin, bringing pots, kettles, vases, boxes, scraps of paper, or cloth, and in fact everything they could find that was movable, adding much to the Coolie's apparent perplexity with their constant cries of "Take this!" "Do you want that?" "Shall I pack this in?" &c., &c. Meantime the puzzled emigrant looked first at one thing and then at another, and before he could fully decide whether he wished to take one article his attention was called away by the introduction of several others, keeping him always busy, and yet accomplishing nothing. His officious relatives would fill the baskets with trash that he could never use, and when he discovered that all his baggage room was thus occupied he would scold at a furious rate, and with unmistakable gestures command the instant removal of the undesirable rubbish. Old shoes that the family had long before thrown aside as useless were carefully wrapped in clean paper and placed near the baskets, as if the assistants thought that old clothes could be worn in America which had been discarded in China. These bundles the Coolie was obliged personally to undo before he knew what they contained, so that much of his time was employed in taking off the wrappers and indignantly throwing away such useless and worthless articles as the busy family exhumed from the dark and unfrequented corners of the cabin. At one time he had a barber shaving his forehead, a friend braiding his long cue, his wife darning a hole in his loose pantaloons, and was himself trying to pack three quarts of rice-flour into a single quart box. The barber spattered the lather and pulled his hair, the wife pricked him with her needle, the flour flew in every direction, while the motion of his head made an interminable snarl of the half-braided cue. Everybody attempted to talk at once, each person shouting at the top of his voice; until there was such a din as to drown even the voices of the squalling children. Their grief, however, was sufficiently apparent in their contorted and tear-streaked faces. The pigs squealed and dashed recklessly back and forth through the crowd, the hens cackled and flew upon the roof of the cabin, while one venturesome old cock stood upon the ridgepole and crowed as if he was sounding a fire alarm. At last the Coolie escaped from the barber, and, out of patience with his hindersome neighbors, he overturned the baskets and dashed their contents on the ground. Meal and flour packages, papers of salt, and bottles of various liquids, broke by the fall and melting into each other, formed a compound more difficult of analysis than the famous life-preserver of Doctor Van Erkin. His bewildered looks, as he beheld the ruin his haste had caused, were even more strange than the compound at his feet. For a moment he gazed as if he was unable to realize the exact condition of things, and then in another outburst of anger he further demolished the curious heap by giving it several powerful kicks. Here the friendly assembly interfered, and each one caught up some of the flying packages and preserved them from impending demolition. The Coolie grew a little calmer, and, replacing the pole upon the balance-stick, began his preparations anew, this time unassisted by his offended neighbors. Placing each soiled bundle in a new wrapper, he packed them carefully away in the baskets, economizing every inch of room, until he had crowded them almost to bursting. Still there were many things left. Bundles of joss-sticks, and little piles of sugar-cane, bamboo fans, and ebony chop-sticks, tin platters and porcelain teacups, with innumerable parcels of clothing and eatables, called for transportation and there was no room. Finally, after discarding a book to make room for the dice-box, and, leaving behind a fan in place of the dominos he took, he discarded the unpacked goods and tied a paper over the baskets. His wife then took down the partially dried clothes and tied them in a bundle for the Coolie to carry under his arm. The preparations were then complete; and after patting the cheeks of his wife and children, and bowing low to all his friends, he shouldered his burden and hastened toward Hongkong.

The Coolie in the interior who makes the same preparations and experiences the same perplexities has seen only the lightest part of his labor when the baskets are packed. He has a long journey before him through a country without stages, carriages, or cars, and where banditti lurk in every corner to rob or carry away the defenceless traveller. If, as we have supposed, his cabin is situated on the shore of a long river-like arm of the sea, he may manage to secure a boat to take him a part of the way on his journey. But, even then, unless he occupies many days in sailing around the peninsulas, he will have a walk before him, which, with his heavy-loaded baskets, will put his strength to a severe test. In the northern provinces they use a kind of one-wheeled cart or wheelbarrow, to which they attach sails, and trimming them to the wind manage to make the air push the load along while the Coolie walks behind and steers with the handles, just as he would without the sail.

This kind of a sail-wheelbarrow is sometimes seen in the lower provinces, especially when a laborer has a heavy load to carry a long distance. An instance where an emigrant rigged up a wheelbarrow after the European pattern and put it under sail was related to me by some of the English residents of Swatow, and so striking was its originality that I have made it the subject of an illustration.* The Coolie travelled four hundred and twenty miles with the wheelbarrow and sail, having on board over two hundred pounds of baggage, a part of which he was obliged to sell after his arrival at Swatow to secure his passage to Salem, Oregon.

But whether the Coolie about whom we write is obliged to carry his baggage with pole and baskets, stow it away in a wheelbarrow with sails, or takes it to the port by boat, we will not stop now to inquire; but will suppose that he accomplishes the task unmolested by robbers or government officers and will leave him, at the end of this chapter, just entering the English colony of Hongkong.

* Frontispiece.

CHAPTER XVI.

BURIAL INSURANCE.

Secret Societies in China. — Opposing Taxation. — Organized "Strikes." — The Effect of Strikes in China. — Insurance Associations. — Insuring to Members a Safe Voyage, and a Burial in China. — Embalming the Dead. — Returning Bodies from the United States. — The "Companies" in California. — Their Objects, &c. — The Coolie's Last Respects to Boodah.

THE Chinese as a people have a special liking for mysterious rites and strange ceremonials, and this feeling has given rise to a great many secret societies, clans, and brotherhoods, in which candidates for initiation are passed through severe tests and symbolic manœuvres. Like the Free Masons and Odd Fellows of the United States, these societies have no connection whatever with government, although the object to be attained by the Chinese associations is far different from that of the American societies, or lodges. The former are for the purpose of mutual protection against oppression or for united aggressive movements of an immoral kind, while the latter aim at the inculcation of the soundest principles of morality and brotherly love. There are a great many associations in China which are not secret, although they are exclusive, and many of them have a noble object; such as the promotion of the arts and sciences, and the perfection of members in the literature of the Empire. These, however, are confined to the wealthy and literary classes, whose education and easy circumstances incline them toward the discipline of the mind. Among the laboring people — between whom and the wealthy there is such a great gulf — there are but a very few organizations that have not for their object either the protection of their property or members or the fraudulent possession of their neighbor's goods. Sometimes the Coolies band together and resist the tax-collector or sheriff, and as the government dare not provoke rebellion by punishing so many evil-doers at once, the Coolies usually accomplish the double purpose of venting their spite upon an obnoxious officer, and escaping the payment of reasonable taxes, which at first they had been willing to pay. The clans that capture so many of the prisoners who are sold to the Portuguese "Coolie traders" are usually a kind of secret family organizations, the purpose of which is to exterminate the family of some enemy. The fact that they roam about in the light of day, killing and destroying without the interference of the authorities, shows the inefficiency of the government and the carelessness of the people. Another kind of a secret society is that entered into by laborers to induce an advance in their wages. This is in every way a counterpart of the organized "strikes" of the Crispins, miners, printers, &c. of America, and shows the *natural* independence of the Chinese mind. But they seldom accomplish anything permanent. Perhaps a continued secret annoyance, or a threatened calamity from a body of men, the numbers and character of which is unknown to him, may induce the capitalist to raise their pay for a few weeks in order that he may get his money out of the business, and invest it elsewhere, but beyond that nothing has been done; of which the present low rate of wages is good evidence. For two thousand years the laborers have been "striking," burning, murdering, and otherwise misbehaving themselves, yet they are as much oppressed as ever, and the rate of wages now is not over five or six cents a day. The capitalists have become too much afraid of "strikes" to invest in manufacturing enterprises, and high and low, rich and poor, suffer in consequence.

Marketmen or merchants dealing in the same articles often combine, and in secret conclave resolve the price up or down, at the same time setting afloat such rumors, or adopting such deceitful behavior as will create a demand for their merchandise. Thus it will be seen that the Chinese were "Crispins," "Sons of Labor," &c., and formed trade combinations and monopolies a thousand years or more before America was discovered. Insurance associations, by the terms of which assistance is rendered to any member in case of accident, either to his property, family, or himself, are often found; and even among the very poorest population such associations are flourishing and beneficial. They are, however, usually under the directorship of some wealthy or educated person, who attends to the duties of the company for a fixed and liberal salary. They insure each other's crops, animals, and clothing, and unite in the expenses when a relative of any member dies. It is said that they insure poor young men a happy marriage, and take risks on the sex of an unborn child, each member paying his share of a loss, on the "mutual" plan.

Since the emigration to America became so active, a variety of societies have been organized for the purpose of insuring to the emigrant a successful trip, sound health, or a safe return. These, it is said, did a great business at one time, but owing to the difficulty of collecting premiums from members, or dues from the company in case of loss, they have nearly all died out. Out of these has sprung another, which, as it is founded on a much firmer basis than its predecessors, may enjoy a longer and more prosperous life. It is called by Europeans the "Burial Insurance Company." Just how a candidate for membership is initiated, or on what terms he is admitted, is not known outside, owing to the secrecy of the proceedings. Its members are so bound by oaths or contracts that they have been known to deny the very existence of the society, the benefits of whose care they shortly after received. Enough is seen of it, however, to know that the body of any member who dies abroad will be brought home at the expense of the society, and buried with his ancestors. The agents of the company make it a part of the contract, when procuring passage tickets for members, that, in case of death on board, the shipmaster shall embalm and send home the body. It is supposed that each member is the authorized agent of the company, in case of a death, and all of his expenses in attending to the transportation of the body on land or water, with the cost of embalming, is paid promptly upon the receipt of his bill in Hongkong. This society also cares for the bodies of men who are not members, and has made a contract with the steamships and other vessels that ply between San Francisco and Hongkong, the terms of which place the captain and surgeon of each ship under obligation to embalm and bring to Hongkong the body of *every* Chinaman who dies upon the ship. The usual price paid for this service is twenty-five or thirty dollars. When the body of a man is received who has no certificate of membership, the company pays the charges, and, adding its fees, sends the bill with the body to the town where live the friends of the deceased. The party having charge of the body is instructed not to deliver it until the bill is paid or ample security given for its future settlement. As the secretary keeps a record of all who emigrate from that port, with the address of their relatives, he cannot fail to find the family; and as the friends would make any sacrifice rather than suffer the spirit to curse them for the neglect of the body, they manage in some way to pay the company's account, and bury the remains according to their superstitious customs.

It often happens that the Coolie has not sufficient time between the hour of his arrival at Hongkong and the departure of the vessel to secure the benefits of this insurance, or it may be that he sails from some other port where "burial insurance" is unknown. Such being the case, he accomplishes the same purpose by joining one of the "companies" in California. Although the objects of these companies are manifold; being a warehouse for storing baggage, a bank for the deposit of gold and silver, a hotel and assembly hall, as well as a charitable institution to such as are needy, and hence a membership would be desirable even to the previously insured, yet one of its most prominent objects is the guaranty to its members of a grave among their ancestors. The Coolie who pays ten dollars as an initiation fee, and keeps his yearly dues to the company settled in advance, will not only be protected in his rights, during his stay in America, but in case of death will be carried by the agents of the company to his old home in China, and there interred with all the ceremonials of his superstitious creed. It has been stated that these companies were immoral, intriguing political institutions, organized, like many in China, to shield criminals from the penalties of crime, or to put money in the pockets of the members without regard for honesty or humanity. Others have enthusiastically leaped at the conclusion that they were charitable institutions, and consequently placed a high estimate upon the charitable tendency of the Chinese character. The fact is, however, as I have ascertained from its officers and members, that these "companies" were instituted by a few of the educated classes who came over to make money by looking after the welfare of their less informed countrymen. The plan was a shrewd and a wise one, as the benefits they confer and the profits they return have long since established. Whether the originators, who are the officers, receive anything more than their salaries — a hundred dollars a month or less — I have not been able to ascertain, although the company has an income which must largely exceed the expenses. The establishment of such institutions for financial gain does not in any way detract from their general usefulness, and I presume that, as a reputation for charity increases the business of the company, the officers would be glad of an opportunity to show that feature of their enterprise in its strongest light. If, as it very seldom happens, a Coolie dies in California or Oregon, who does not belong to either of the "companies," the members or officers of the nearest one, usually undertake the task of sending the body home, with the hope of obtaining pay of the friends, in the same way that the insurance society of Hongkong collects its bills. But if it should happen that the deceased comes from a part of the Chinese Empire that has not a sufficient number of representatives in California to make the organization of a "company" profitable, he will be buried by the organization whose members come from the district nearest to his native province, and the expense, should the deceased be poor, will be charged in the general expenses.

But little is known of these companies, among the unsophisticated Coolies in China, who are just starting for America, and as they cannot stop for a single night at any of the Hongkong boarding-houses, without meeting with the runners of the company, we will suppose that the Coolie we have followed thus far goes through the initiatory ordeal, and comes out of the office well assured that his body will be looked after, should his spirit abandon it in the wilds of America. His next step will be toward the furniture shop of Lei-Sing or Chee-Ling, where he purchases a straw or grass mattress, provided the ship does not furnish it, for his bunk in the vessel, and provided he has money enough left to do so. This he orders to be sent with his baggage on board the ship, or leaves it at the shop until his return, and goes down the "Queen's road," through a part of "China town," to pay his last respects to Boodah. In a "temple," or other shed covered with carved dragons, of hideous designs, behind a highly ornamented altar, sits the idol in a dusty cloud of paper drapery. Before it the Coolie prostrates himself, and prays for a prosperous voyage. Then rising to his feet, pulls out a joss-stick from the bundle near the throne of the idol, and, finding it a lucky, or affirmative one, he cheerfully dons his umbrella-hat and marches back to the steamboat wharf.

CHAPTER XVII.

THE SHIP.

A Pacific Mail Steamship. — The Coolie's Surprise at the Accommodations. — Examination before the Consul. — Departure from Hongkong. — Games and Gambling. — The Food. — Smoking Opium. — Deaths on Steamers. — The Refusal of Sick Chinamen to take Medicine. — Incident where the Relatives of an Invalid attempt to frighten away the bad Spirits. — Sailing Vessels. — Deaths from bad Food and Ventilation. — Arrival in San Francisco. — Meeting with old Friends.

ONE who has seen those palace steamships owned by the Pacific Mail Steamship Company, plying between Hongkong, Yokohama, and San Francisco, can form some idea of the astonishment with which the Coolie first walks their decks. Never, perhaps, having seen a European steamer, and having pictured in his imagination a vessel a little larger and very similar to the native junks which plough the inland waters with such ludicrous awkwardness, he will look with wonder when, for the first time, he sees the trim masts, broad decks, glistening machinery, and comfortable cabins of the American steamers. Used to the

"NO MUCHEE WALKEE." — Page 256.

yells, creaks, and gongs of the native barks, he will be almost oppressed with the silence that reigns on board of those well-ordered vessels. Instead of the mere chance to lie down upon deck, or the little dark corner into which he may crawl in very stormy weather, he is shown through a long corridor of neatly kept sleeping-apartments, and is, at last, much to his surprise, shown one in which he is expected to make his bed. Such a sleeping-room as the one he is given not even a mandarin or a governor on shore could ever exhibit! With a light heart he deposits his baggage, and, thinking what a beautiful country America must be, if its ships are any index of the dwellings on shore, he wanders up and down the deck through the by-ways and avenues of that floating city, greeting old acquaintances or making new ones among the thousand other Coolies which are to keep him company. Then — if he has not already passed the ordeal at the harbor-master's office on shore — comes the doctors, consuls, and local officials, to test his health and prove his "free will," as well as to secure to him plenty of room, with food and care. In long rows the Chinamen file by the examining surgeon, who, if he sees an unhealthy Coolie, about whose safe passage there is any doubt, he orders him ashore to await the healing of his wounds or the termination of his disease. Then appears the first official representative of the "flowery flag" which the Coolie has ever seen, in the person of the United States Consul. And before this august personage he is stopped by the local officials, and through an interpreter is requested to respond to the following questions: —

"What is your name?"

"Arr Sing."

"Where do you come from?"

"Shanking."

"Where are you going?"

"To the United States."

"What are you going for?"

"To work."

"Who induced you to go?"

"No one."

"Why do you go?"

"Because I wish to get higher wages and be a free man."

"Who sold you your ticket?"

"The elder."

"Did you sign any contract to work in America in payment for the ticket?"

"No."

"Have you made *any* agreement with regard to your labor after arrival in California?"

"No."

"Then you declare unqualifiedly that you are under no obligations whatever to any person or persons, which will bind you to labor for any particular party in the United States?"

"I do."

One after another his countrymen file by and answer these queries, and, while he stands wondering why the "Melican" is so anxious that he should be free before he leaves China, there is a sudden stir and bustle on board, the bell sounds a warning, the visitors and officials hurry down the side, the harbor boats pull away from the eddy of the wheels, and with a slight tremor the great puffing, flag-decked leviathan swings from the buoy and glides down the harbor, bound for America.

During those long dull days which follow, when there is but a barren "waste of waters" without, and a tedious routine of eating, walking, sleeping, within, the Coolie occupies nine tenths of his time in thinking and planning what he shall do with the remaining one tenth. His love for games of chance brings out the dice, dominos, cards, and numerous other gaming toys which the European looker-on has never before seen. Owing to the crowded state of the deck, but a small proportion can play at one time; and with a polite regard for each other's feelings, they often exchange. Scarce a day passes without an opportunity being given each Coolie to lose or win a dollar or two in play. The game is usually played upon the floor of a lower deck, with the participants seated around in a circle, and with a crowd of spectators standing by, eager to censure or praise each move or throw of their champion. Sometimes the spectators become so interested in the game that hundreds neglect their meals in order to see it finished, and often sit in the dark on the edge of their beds, long after retiring hours, discussing what might have been if Too Ling or Arr Hoo had made such and such a move.

Their meals are composed almost exclusively of rice; although, if they should desire it, the steward would supply them with meat and vegetables. They eat as they play; seated upon the floor with a huge pan of rice before them, out of which "a division" of ten or twelve skilfully extract enough to appease their appetites by means of those puzzling substitutes for the knife and fork, — the chop-sticks.

Some few smokers, whose sensibilities have not become so dulled as to prevent their securing a passage, pass the tedious hours in the steerage smoking-room, taking in the deadening fumes of opium. This smoking-room is simply a large iron box, fire-proof, and almost air-tight. It will hold several persons when packed full, and is situated in the centre of the forecastle deck, with plenty of room for promenading upon either side. It is supplied with candles or torches, and sometimes with pipes and opium. There, in that dark prison where the uninitiated would suffocate in a few minutes, these devotees of opium stretch themselves out upon the shelves, place a drop of the narcotic liquid in the long pipe, and, holding the bowl in the flame of the candle, puff themselves into blissful insensibility. It often happens that a poor inconsiderate inebriate inhales a drop too much, or the state of his system is such that he drowses beyond the time to which nature limits him, and then he is found pale and lifeless by some official or friend who goes to wake him. The drug-dreamer is dead, and out of the world which has no attraction for him. Well might humanitarians rejoice if he was the only one concerned. But when his embalmed body, — its veins filled with the surgeon's "preservative," — shall be carried with its swollen features into the old hovel, where the family are, upon whom he gave a mortgage to secure his passage, what will be their feelings ?

Deaths on the steamers are not very frequent, as none but healthy persons are allowed to go on board ; yet if a Coolie is taken sick with any serious disease he is almost sure to die. He will never take a dose prescribed by the ship-surgeon, or by any European physician. When told that he must soon die if he does not take the prepared draught, he will smile in derision, as much as to say, "How silly you are to suppose that your draught will circumvent the decree of the Gods !" Sometimes a Chinaman is seized with the cramp, or some spasmodic ailment which a simple draught of *stimulus* would instantly dispel, but he prefers the excrutiating pain and a horrible death to the life-giving potion which he is urged to accept.

I once witnessed an attempt of some inexperienced Coolies to cure a sick person who, owing to his stubborn refusal to take medicine, had been given over by the surgeon of the ship; and, although the ceremony was a torture to the patient, it seemed so much like a burlesque that I laughed in spite of myself. The sick man was afflicted with the colic in connection with an attack of the erysipelas, and was on his side lying doubled up, with his knees under his chin, and the side of his swollen face upon the cold, damp deck. He had been advised by the physician to apply a warm poultice to the face, with a very warm internal dose of whiskey and cayenne-pepper. But positively refusing to take the prescription, the sufferer, between his groans, expressed a desire that his countrymen would drive away the *bad spirits* that were afflicting him. It might be that the souls of some enemies, or of some relatives whom the invalid had failed to supply with spiritual money, had taken this method of showing their spite or dissatisfaction. They could be frightened away if the crew and passengers would only make noise enough. So the superstitious Coolies gathered up all the bamboo hats, pieces of board, tin plates, pans, and iron kettles that could be found, and, led by a sailor with a gong, they formed a circle around the colic-stricken Coolie and began to thump upon them with chop-sticks, canes, and belaying-pins. Such a din! It would have made an invalid of the least indisposed, and its effect upon a man with a severe head and stomach ache was doubtless torture to which the rack would have been a pleasure. Yet he bore it with remarkable fortitude, while the players applied themselves to their thumping with an earnestness that bade fair to give them the colic, cholera, or cramp, as a result of over-exertion and consequent perspiration. They rattled away until the captain, at the request of the deafened passengers, ordered them to stop; and then they anxiously inquired of the patient if the bad spirits were gone. His answer, half shriek, half groan, with contortions and kicks, would convince the most sceptical that, whatever the influence which was giving him such misery, it had not been scared away. So they began to run around him and beat the air with their sticks and pans, in the hope that their random thrusts might happen to punch the ribs, or their unresisted blows fall on the heads, of such devils as happened to be hovering around. This striking and thrusting they kept up for a half-hour, when, seeing that the spirits still kept hold of the sufferer, they resorted to other methods. Securing a number of glass goblets of the steward, they placed them in two rows around the sick man, and placing three or four burning joss-sticks in each, they began to chant some formula in a monotonous tone, keeping time with the clapping of their hands. They had hardly begun this ceremony, however, before a pang more acute than usual seized the patient, and with a sudden kick and a roll he overturned the clinking goblets, and scattered the joss-sticks in every direction. This was considered as an ill omen, and gathering up the glassware, and stamping out the fire of the sticks, these idolatrous physicians took up the man and carried him to the cabin; where it was said they made offerings to the gods, in the shape of plates of rice, and then left him to die. His body was afterward embalmed and taken ashore at Manilla.

In the well-regulated Pacific Mail Steamships such exhibitions are rarely permitted, and if the friends of a sick person wish to drive away the "bad spirits," they usually attempt it in some quiet way which does not attract the attention of the "barbarians." In fact, the number of deaths on the Eastward passage is astonishingly small, when we consider the immense number who are brought over by the steamers of that company. The accommodations and sanitary regulations are so perfect, and the room for deck exercise so ample, that the Coolie is in a much healthier condition, usually, when he arrives in San Francisco than when he leaves Hongkong. This is not always the case with the sailing-vessels which make a business of importing Coolies, and, in some instances, a large percentage have died from the effects of bad food and insufficient ventilation. The law of the United States has so regulated the emigrant traffic, that a United States Consul will not clear a vessel that is crowded beyond a healthy and comfortable limit. But many sailing-vessels after obtaining a clearance from the Consul-General at Hongkong, heave-to in the straits below that city and take on board a large number of Coolies, sent down in small boats for that purpose. The Coolies have no thought of disease, and willingly crowd into the vessel as long as the officers will receive them. It is in the interest of the owners of such ships, that the false circulars, elsewhere referred to, are sent into the country, while the food and accommodations which the passengers get may be said to be in an inverse ratio to the alluring promises made to them in the placards.

But whether in sailing-vessel or steamer, in a dark hold or in a cheerful cabin, it matters not to the Coolie, when he has arrived safely at the "Golden Gate" of San Francisco harbor. There the Coolie shows an eagerness to reach the shore which does not characterize his action when returning to China. The great dreaded ocean is passed, and the land of freedom and of gold lies just before him. He imagines that now the hopes long cherished are about to be realized, and it is with great impatience that he waits for the mooring. Many of his too impatient countrymen leap into the water in the narrow straits and strike out for the shore, or for the boats of relatives alongside, while in some ships the whole load has disappeared before the slow vessel has thrown its hawsers to the wharf. This ungovernable desire to stand on American soil, and to begin the work which the Coolie truly believes is to emancipate him from all ills, is often an advantage to the owners of an overcrowded vessel, who wish to avoid the penalties that the government officers would attach to the ship for their disregard of the United States law. Their ships always go into the dock with a *less* number than they had on board when the consul gave them clearance papers; meantime the happy Coolie, the fresher for his bath, and the happier to see shore, because of his hardships on board, is taken in hand by the agents of the "Chinese Companies," and sitting down at the club-house, in a large circle of friends, who wish to hear the news from home, he eats his rice, sips his tea, and tells of the circulars, the answer of the gods, the visit to the elder, the reception of his ticket, his packing up, the journey to Hongkong, and the voyage across the Pacific; and when the sands of his story, with those of the hour-glass, have wholly run out, he turns upon his listeners and anxiously INQUIRES FOR WORK.

CHAPTER XVIII.

SOLD FOR DEBT.

Chinese Slavery. — Difference between a Free Coolie and a Bondman. — Treatment of Slaves. — The Sale of Men, Women, and Children. — Infanticide. — Sale of Daughters for doubtful Purposes. — The Coolie's Failure to pay his Note. — The Mortgage on the Family Foreclosed. — How the Sale is conducted. — Frequency of these Sales. — Selling Children to buy Passage Tickets.

IT has often been stated by writers upon China, that slavery in that country was a very "mild form of servitude"; and their conclusion is usually reached by a comparison of the Coolie in a state of slavery with his condition before he became a bondman. This would be a correct inference if the previous condition of the Coolie was a state of freedom. For the *status* of a slave in China is but a very little lower than that of the lowest class of free Coolies, while in some instances the former condition is far preferable to the latter. To be a slave is to be the property of some rich man, who, although he has absolute control of the laborer, will take some little care to provide sufficient food and clothing to keep him in a working condition. To be a free laborer is to be subject to the same conditions which hamper the action of a slave, while with the wages he receives, he cannot provide himself with the necessities of life, nor obtain the smallest portion of the care which is bestowed upon the slave. Such being the case the state of absolute slavery is but a single step downward, and has advantages which make it "mild" indeed. But when we consider the condition of the higher classes, whose sons have the advantages of schools and social training, and to whom all the best offices in the Empire are open, and afterward glance down at the degradation which marks the features and behavior of the slave and his children, we will conclude that, instead of being a "mild" state of slavery, it is the very worst. I do not think that it is so severe a blow to the happiness of a person to be sold as a slave, in a country where there are middle classes, the gradations of which fill the wide gap between entire bondage and entire freedom, as it would be in a nation where there are only two classes, — the bond and the free. But this does not make it any the less degrading in its effect upon the physical and mental constitutions of those concerned. The slave in China is whipped, branded, put in stocks and pillories, and otherwise maltreated as often as were the African slaves in the Southern States of the American Union. They have as hard tasks to perform, as little of the luxuries of life, and are nearly as often separated from their families as were the bondmen in the English colonies. There was supposed to be a certain code of morality and Christianity which governed the actions of American masters in their dealings with slaves, and so there is in China; but one is followed at present with just about the same fidelity as that which marked the actions of the *pretended* practisers of the other. In China it is not considered respectable for a master to sell a husband away from his whole family, although the girls may be sold at any time. Neither is it *fashionable* to keep a male slave after he is thirty years of age without purchasing a wife for him. But if native evidence is trustworthy, the observance of this moral law is the exception rather than the rule. The male slave is a valuable piece of property, and the heathen master is more apt to use it in the way which will return the greatest dividend, without regard to morality or suffering, than is the slave-owner in civilized lands.

The worst features of Chinese bondage is seen in the dealings with females. The women in China, among all classes, are at the best but a low order of slaves. They are salable *things*, and the circumstances of the parents always determine their value. If the parents feel at the birth of a daughter that there will not be a demand for girls, owing to the preponderance in the neighborhood of male children, they do not hesitate to strangle or drown the helpless human being who was so unlucky as to be born a female.* In their best estate the girls are uneducated, and consequently immoral; and are treated like useless, intruding dogs until they become grandmothers, when, in accordance with some strange superstition, they are treated with much reverence and generosity. But when a daughter or wife is bought and sold, and simply tolerated as a necessary evil, even in her highest state of freedom, what must be her condition when she becomes a slave? All wives are purchased from their parents, and among the higher classes, are kept in the closest confinement, lest in their ignorance and innocence they become a prey to the arts of some man not their husband. But the female slave, unless fortunately bought for a second or third wife, is not only a concubine or mistress, but also a field-hand, house-servant, and a general drudge. While the wife can only be sold to be the wife of another man, the slave can be, and is, sold for any purpose however vile,

* See verification in Doolittle's "Social Life of the Chinese," Vol. II. p. 203; "Williams's Middle Kingdom," Vol. II. p. 98; Nevins's "China and the Chinese," p. 253.

and has no chance to choose her master or her place of abode. Houses of prostitution are found in every town and village, however small, and city bawdy-houses are almost numberless. These are usually filled with daughters whose fathers sold them into slavery, either on account of poverty or on a mere speculation. The vast number of these houses and the astonishingly low price* which the girls bring in the market is conclusive proof of the great prevalence of this kind of female slavery. No statistics of the number of females purchased for servitude or prostitution have been gathered by Chinese authority, so that all writers have been left to judge by private information, some having placed the number as high as ten per cent of the female population, and others as low as one per cent. But they all agree that in late years it has been surprisingly on the increase. If this is a "mild form of servitude," when compared with the freedom, education, virtue, and refine-

* A handsome girl sixteen years of age will command a price varying from twenty-five dollars to fifty dollars. In case they are sought by Europeans, the price is advanced to accord with the known means of the purchaser. Women with small feet bring more in the native markets, where the buyer wishes for a wife or a mistress, because it is a mark of gentility "to be scarcely able to walk." But as few families of the Coolie class are able to bring up a girl without her assistance, it is a very rare thing to see a Coolie woman with "stunted feet"; and when one is seen, she has been thus maimed merely as a matter of speculation.

ment which characterize the female masses in civilized lands, then I have yet to hear of servitude in a malignant form. It would seem to me to be far more "mild" if the persons bargained away for such labor, or for such vile uses, were the people of an inferior or conquered race, instead of being their own legitimate sons and daughters. Some idea of it can be formed by supposing that Americans should sell their children into bondage, or should, in neighborhood quarrels, exercise a right to sell into slavery all their captives, as is now done in the lower provinces of China. It must be borne in mind that the selling of children, except to be the first wives of neighbor's sons, is confined to the lower classes, and that these slaves are the result of poverty and a lack of refined education among the common people. The care and good training, as well as the ample provisions for the freedom and comfort of their children among the higher classes show how susceptible the Chinese mind is of cultivation, morally as well as intellectually; and that, when left untrammelled, the affections of the Chinese are as strong as those of other nations.

Let us now return to the family of the Coolie whom he left to toil their way through privations, until such a time as he should be able to pay up his indebtedness and send them money. Days, weeks, months pass away and they hear nothing from him. Every morning they all repair to the rice-field and every evening return to their hard couches, waiting, hoping that each hard day's work will be their last. Meantime the Coolie fails to get work, or, having found employment, receives much less wages than he expected; or, perhaps, loses his money by accident or robbery; and cannot meet his note, which has been sent for collection to the office of some Chinese broker in San Francisco. It is said that the Chinese in California and in other colonies gradually become more generous and affectionate toward their relatives, and it would seem to be the natural result of an escape from the soul-breaking servitude which enthralled them in China. If so, then he must feel a grief, which is not allied with pride or superstition when the day draws near — comes — and passes — on which the note should be paid and he knows that his family are to suffer for his failure. Perhaps a few days after he gets the money, and hurrying to the office finds that the note was protested and sent to China by the last steamer, and any remittance to China by the following vessel would be too late to prevent the threatened disaster and too small to redeem them and pay the agent's expenses for so doing. So he abandons the present hope and goes to work with greater zeal and closer economy, determined to go himself at some future time and carry money enough to buy them all back.

Three weeks later the mandarin who purchased the Coolie's ticket before the latter left China receives a formal note from the office in Canton, stating that the Coolie has failed to make payment at the San Francisco office, and consequently the broker at Canton declares the mandarin's note to be due and unpaid. This causes that official to rejoice; for, to the fifty per cent already charged, he can now add another fee, according to his contract with the elder. He therefore sends the money at once and pays the note which he gave for the ticket, together with the interest, and, having made out a bill of heavy fees for this "trouble," notifies the elder that, as the latter's note is now *two months overdue,* it must be paid at once, with the fees just added. This the elder also welcomes as a matter of good luck, as he can also make a heavy charge for his "time," and makes all possible haste to pay the mandarin according to his agreement. Now it becomes his turn to collect, and the family is notified of the Coolie's failure and the consequent liability on the bond. As the note is already *three months overdue,* the elder can proceed to collect or sell at once, and without previous notice; but should he dislike to take the trouble or have the name of being uncharitable, or thinks that the family will not sell for a sufficient amount to settle the whole bill, he gives them a certain time in which to pay the note, and if he sees any way in which he thinks that they may realize the money he makes the suggestion: Perhaps they have clothing or ornaments which they can pawn or sell; perhaps their employer will advance them money rather than lose their labor, or they may have relatives who are able to assist them: under some circumstances the members of the village clan with whom the Coolie is associated will unite in a subscription for the release of the family, and sometimes the priests solicit gifts for the same purpose. But supposing the Coolie to live in an agricultural district where clans and associations are uncommon, and where no clan feuds bind the members of a family together, — all these means fail, and at the end of the stipulated time the elder sends a police-officer with orders to sell such a number, beginning with the girls, as will satisfy his bill and pay the charges of the sale. If the total amount for which the family is liable be over three hundred dollars, — as it is very likely to be, if the cost of the ticket were forty dollars, — it will doubtless be necessary to sell the whole family. But should the police-officer conclude that the price of the girls would be sufficient, he will either bring customers to the house and endeavor to make his bargains there, or he will take the girls into the village, and, placing them in a conspicuous location, post a placard upon their persons declaring them to be "for sale."

This is often done with the whole family; and in some cases, when a sale cannot readily be effected in the native village, the officer marches them to the nearest seaport and endeavors to dispose of them to "Coolie traders" or other European purchasers. In Canton there are one or two companies who make it their entire business to purchase girls at forced sales and keep them until they can dispose of them at an advance. These companies have "runners" or agents, who are usually old women, in the cities of Hongkong, Swatow, Amoy, or Macaow, who find European customers and "guarantee satisfaction." Sailors, and members of the low class which are to be found in every commercial city often purchase such girls, and after a few months or weeks abandon them and go to sea or send them away to give place to others whose faces and ways are more pleasing.

The sale of a family in Canton in the month of April, 1870, will well illustrate what may become of the delinquent Coolie's family in case of a sale under the bond. This family lived in the town of Tsunghwa, and were mortgaged to a broker in Canton, through the mandarin, for the price of the Coolie's tickets and a few unpaid debts left behind. His failure to pay made a foreclosure necessary, and consequently a sale. The vendors having made repeated attempts to sell in Tsunghwa, finally brought the family — mother, two sons, and one daughter — to Canton and exposed them for sale near one of the gates. They were there nearly a week before the first sale was made, and that only included the disposal of the girl to the keeper of a brothel in Hainan for thirty-three dollars and seventy-five cents. Two days after, the youngest son, twelve years of age, was sold to a silk manufacturer among the foreign population of Canton for sixty dollars. The same day the older son, who was eighteen years of age and quite intelligent, attracted the attention of a sea-captain, who, out of compassion, gave seventy-six dollars for the boy and put him on board a vessel loading with Coolies for the southern ports of North America. The extraordinary low price received for the children made the sale of the mother necessary, and, as no Chinaman wanted so old a woman for a wife or mistress, she was purchased by a speculator, and afterwards "let out" to European families as a nurse; and it was from her and the captain that I received the story of the family's misfortune.

Several instances have been known where such families have been purchased by the agents of ships that were waiting for a cargo of Chinese, and sent to America under a written contract to work for the purchaser a certain length of time after their arrival in America; but they were instructed what to say to the Consul, and of course answered in the negative when asked by him if they were under any contract to labor.

These sales for debt, in cases where the Coolie pledges his family for the price of his ticket, cannot be said to be very frequent, although they are much more so now than they have been in past years. To be in danger of separation and slavery usually excites a mortgaged family to great effort, and by begging, working, and stealing they will many times pay off the whole or a part of the debt before the foreclosure; while some Coolies, rather than run the risk of losing the whole, sell some of the children, in the absence of other property, and with the proceeds pay for their tickets in advance. The sales, however, by emigrants to America form but an infinitesimal portion of the great traffic in human flesh, made necessary by poverty and two thousand years of superstitious tyranny.

CHAPTER XIX.

QUERIES.

Growing Desire to reach America. — How many there are coming. — What Classes will soon come. — Why married Women are not brought to the United States. — The Prejudice against Foreigners.

HOW MANY ARE THERE COMING?

Until recently it has required considerable urging on the part of interested foreigners to induce the Chinese to undertake a journey to America; and even as late as 1869–70 circulars and travelling agents were necessary in order to obtain a full cargo of passengers within a reasonable time. This was not owing to the absence of a desire to escape the hardships at home, or, as has often been stated, to a prejudice against the people of our country. This is sufficiently evident from the alacrity with which they responded to every special call, and the activity they displayed in taking advantage of suggestions and means of escape which American contractors gave them. Their habitual subserviency and deference to the laws and officials of China, their uncertainty with regard to the truth of the representations made to them, as well as their natural pride in everything connected with their own country, caused them to hesitate and often to reject the offers of passage and work when coming from the most trustworthy establishments. But the opening of China to foreign trade, with the consequent contact with the agents of American commercial houses, has a tendency to enlighten the working people upon the subject of emigration.

The establishment of a steamship line, reducing the length of a passage more than two thirds, and the influence of its many well-treated employees,* has also done much toward breaking the old ties and expanding the ideas of the serving classes. The wholesome fear with which the government officials regard the American navy, and their consequent hesitancy in interfering with any traffic in which American vessels are engaged, gives the Coolie an opportunity to leave the country in United States vessels, when he could not go in those of Spain or Portugal. These fresh inducements and opportunities, combined with those to which reference has been made, have at last turned the scale; and now, instead of shipmasters searching for passengers, the passengers are searching for shipmasters.

* The common sailors on the Pacific Mail Steamship Company's vessels are all Chinese.

To those who have watched the course of events, the steadily decreasing prejudice of the laboring classes has been a matter of much interesting study. At first it was almost impossible to obtain a Coolie for this continent, by fair means; and it was necessary to go with weapons of war in order to get a full cargo for Cuba. Afterward promises of riches and comforts were made, which were as astonishing, no doubt, to the contractors as to the Coolie; but even with such prizes before them, very few could break through their crusted custom and accept the offer, which they all believed to be made in good faith. Later, such promises were accepted, and the Coolie trade grew in spite of the rumors that the Chinaman had been enslaved. Still later, the national prejudices were so far overcome that a large number were found willing to emigrate, with the prospect only of reasonable wages and the comforts of life, and now they begin to crowd into seaports, and patiently wait for the departure of ships, having endured many privations, and run many risks to get their tickets; all without even an offer of work when they shall arrive in the United States. This is a very different spirit from that displayed twenty years ago, and a contemplation of its future effect upon our country leads us into a labyrinth of perplexity out of which we cannot at present see our way. All these years the circulars, "runners," rumors, and returners have been exercising an almost imperceptible, but yet powerful, influence upon the opinions and behavior of the Chinese; and now it appears as if the necessity for such agencies for the purpose of inducing emigration has entirely ceased. At present it does not require anything but a notice that the American-bound ship will leave the port at a certain time to fill its spare space with anxious Coolies. If this feeling of confidence, which it has taken so long to substitute in the place of narrow prejudice, shall continue to increase year by year, until confidence shall quicken into a desire to come as great as at first was their aversion to such a removal, then we may have as many million a year coming across to us from China as there are tens of thousands now.

The higher classes will never come so long as the present form of government remains as it is. They possess more wealth, have more privileges, and it may be a better education, than they would enjoy in America. For they not only have all their own rights, such as they would claim under a democratic form of government, but also the rights which in justice belong to the poorer and lower classes. Within twelve months there has been a large emigration from among the middle classes,— such as merchants, clerks, writers, money-changers, and stock-brokers, — and in a few years America may get some of the *literati*, provided that the flood continues. But the governing people, who furnish China with her wonderful laws, histories, schools, &c., and from whom nearly every official visitor gets his good opinion of China, will stay where their prosperity is so great, until some revolution among the oppressed masses shall send them into exile.

WHY DO NOT THE MARRIED WOMEN COME TO THE UNITED STATES?

The laws of China, or rather the will of the officials, will not permit a wife to leave China under any conditions. If any succeed in escaping from the interior to the loading vessel, they do so at the risk of severe punishment, and a life of slavery; and even should the mandarin or elders be willing to connive at their departure as they do at the exodus of the Coolies, their husbands might be obliged to use them as security for borrowed money, or perhaps could not afford to bear the expense of two tickets. If a man should bring his wife to the United States, all the profit she would be to him must accrue from her labor, and that is exceedingly uncertain, while if he brings his slave or mistress he can sell her, or "bind her out" for *any* purpose, should his necessities require it. The men come to America simply to get money and escape present ill, and not to live as they would at home; and they consider their stay too limited to warrant the transfer of a family even if they could do so.

WHY DO THE CHINESE ENTERTAIN SUCH A PREJUDICE AGAINST FOREIGNERS?

Their rigid adherence to custom and their great pride lead them to look with disrespect upon any person, Chinaman or European, who does not behave or believe as they do. Added to this is the very bad record which foreigners have made in the Chinese ports, with regard to honesty and humanity. So much have the people been swindled, and so often have they been maltreated by Europeans, that they would begin to hate them, had there been love before instead of prejudice. To this Americans seem to be considered as exceptions, however little they may deserve it.

Among the ruling class there is a feeling that the presence of foreigners, who hire the lower class, is giving the latter too much independence; and knowing that the growth of this spirit bodes the overthrow of their rule, they lose no opportunity to feed the Coolie's prejudices, and, with their tyrannical power, set him upon deeds of blood for which they themselves dare not be responsible. Oftentimes this hatred is said to be "general," when perhaps it is confined entirely to some mandarin who commands a cringing and thoughtless populace.

SKETCHES.

SKETCHES.

NUMBER ONE.

A Chinese School upon an American Plan.

WE had seen Chinese schools in which all the children chanted their lessons aloud, without regard to unison or harmony; but none of these institutions were conducted on the "American plan." They were purely, awkwardly native: they lacked the democratic and thinking qualities that characterize the schools of America. So we looked forward with great interest to our contemplated visit to a school the teacher of which was a returned California miner, and who prided himself upon the introduction of the "Melican plan." His school was in the second story of a long row of rickety buildings in the north-eastern portion of Hongkong; and while attempting to find it we blundered into the markets, kitchens, sitting-rooms, and pantries of several Chinese tenements, whose half-dressed occupants eyed us with suspicion, and sometimes with anger. But happening to see several urchins who had the thoughtful air of students enter a grocery-shop, carrying Chinese books rolled under their arms, we followed them into the store-room, and through it to a dark, narrow staircase in the farther corner. We knew that the school held its session over this store by the awful din which we had heard without, — rising and falling at intervals like a powerful church-organ. But so obscure and narrow was the staircase we sought that we could not see it, even when we followed close on the heels of the gaudily attired urchins. They disappeared in the dark, and so did we. Walking "by faith and not by sight" was intended to apply solely to spiritual matters, as we were ready to declare, when, after creeping along the stairs, we crushed our hats against the ceiling and barked our shins against projecting beams. For a while the little patter of clogged feet above us indicated the direction which we should take; but at last the noise ceased altogether, and we were left, without a guide, to grope along the darkest and most irregular staircase that it was ever my lot to climb. The roar of the school voices seemed farther away than ever, and beginning to think that we had made a mistake, we stopped to discuss the propriety of proceeding any farther. Just then a wide door but a few feet from us swung suddenly open letting into the passage a blinding flood of light, and an almost deafening jargon of children's voices. It was some seconds before we could see; but when our eyes became a little accustomed to the light, we found ourselves near the highest stair, and gazing point-blank into the school-room for which we had been searching. The door had been opened by one of the scholars within to admit those whom we followed, and the little usher stared with astonishment to see two Europeans rising into the lighted door-way like shadowy ghosts from Hades. "*Hoy tsac!* Hoy tsac*!*" (Pirates!) screamed the startled boys near the door, attempting by gesticulation and shrieks to call the attention of the master. But it would have been utterly useless to make gestures or utter the shrillest screams in a place like that, even were the house on fire.

The room was about twenty feet square, and ceiled at the sides and overhead with planed boards, after the style of some European houses. But the walls were blank and bare, save where some "Americanized" youngster had daubed the walls with grotesque images in crayon. Little mats of bamboo dotted the floor, upon which the scholars sat or stood and repeated their lessons, while a class of little philosophers stood in a row near the centre of the room reciting to the master. As the general appearance of the school was similar to that of others which I had seen, I began a close scrutiny to discover any traits or indications of the boasted "American plan." Several very small boys were engaged in whisking their little cues about each other's heads, by standing back to back, and, jerking their heads from one side to the other, snapping the cue about like a teamster's whip. Two near the door had tied these appendages together, and were pulling with wonderful fortitude to see which would drag the other. One great awkward fellow was rolling up paper balls to fling at the heads of the studiously inclined, while another was cutting a picture of the master in the floor with the aid of a Yankee jackknife. Some were lying flat upon their breasts with a sheet of brown paper before them, upon which they were drawing Chinese letters, and others had manuscript rolls, or books from which they learned to read. But whatever their occupation, — in mischief or out, — standing or seated, — they kept up the constant and boisterous repetition of their lessons, combining study and play in a manner of which American scholars never dreamed.

The master, a large bony-framed man, whose gray cue dragged upon the floor, had so far Americanized his ideas as to wear enormous spectacles, and "beat time" with a bamboo rod which he held in his right hand. When we first saw him he was standing before the class, with one foot upon the only stool (or little bench) which the place afforded, holding his book in his left hand at arm's length,—somewhat higher than his head,—and gazing intently at it under his spectacles and swinging his baton with threatening vigor. With proud tossings of his head and emphatic stampings with the foot upon the stool, he growled out his sentences in the coarsest bass, to which the class responded with the most piercing treble. How he could hear the responses to his questions, or understand what he was saying himself in that uproar, was a mystery. But I suppose he had become so accustomed to the noise that it did not interfere at all with his hearing. His dress was in keeping with his manners. His long blue frock, that fell below the knees, was patched in the sleeves, and shorter on the left side than on the other, while the right leg of his loose pantaloons came but little below the knee, making a strange contrast with the other, that almost hid his left foot. On one foot he had a very large European-made boot, and upon the other a tiny Chinese slipper. His appearance seemed the more awkward from the comparison which the spectator would naturally make between his dress and the neat little blue or black frocks and flowing pantaloons of the scholars.

At the time we entered he was too busily engaged with the lesson and too intent upon it to notice us, and we stood for some moments spreading terror among a score or more of pupils, before his eyes wandered far enough from the book to see us. When he did become conscious of our presence, however, he hastily pulled off his spectacles and placed them under his arm, and, advancing through and over the crowd of boys, shook hands with us and invited us to a seat upon his footstool. I suppose that he said he was glad to see us, and made apologies for the appearance of the school, as his lips moved and face smiled; but not a word could we hear. Our presence seemed to have a stimulating effect upon the whole school, for their guttural *thugs* and chilling falsettos were more excruciating than ever. The master, too, assumed his most dignified attitudes, and summoned up class after class with pompous wavings of his stick, and, having heard — i. e. seen by the movements of their lips — their recital of the lessons given out the day before, would make them repeat after him the sentences of the new lesson until they could remember them. He then sent them away to keep up the senseless repetition until school was closed. His books were filled with extracts from the writings of Confucius and from Chinese history, with a few essays, written by himself or by some of his friends, upon the filial duty of children; and the *words* were taught without explanation or discussion. He had a class in English, but they were away at the time of our visit.

Before the close of the school my friend began to fear that he should be called upon to make "a few remarks" to the scholars, as this was supposed to be an Americanized institution; and he thought that it was an oversight to come there without having previously written, corrected, learned by heart, and practised a speech, with which to bore the scholars when "surprised" by the teacher's request. He wished to know how it would do for him to say that he "expected to see all these boys George Washingtons or Abraham Lincolns," and that, as the most mischievous schoolboys always make the greatest men, he "would advise them to pay strict attention to their studies" and avoid being bothered in old age with office and honors? But the crack of the master's stick against the wall and the sudden rush of the children for the dark stairway quieted the fears of my companion and gave us a model example of the way in which to close a school. After the little cues and sparkling eyes had all disappeared, we asked the master what difference there was between his "plan" and that of other Chinese schools. To which he answered, after telling what he himself had learned in California, that he liked very much to make all "piecie boy belong free," which means that he permitted the boys to do just as they chose in school and out, provided that they paid sufficient attention to their studies to get their lessons. But he incidentally added that it was also his intention to follow the American standard farther and teach them to "muchee big talkee, and likee dat piecie dollar."

NUMBER TWO.

JOKING CHINAMEN.

IT has been said that a Chinaman is not capable of making or appreciating a good joke, but to prove the contrary it is only necessary to begin upon them in a situation where there is no fear of consequences. It was my good fortune to have for a travelling companion, during the greater part of my stay in China, a rollicking, fun-loving, practical-joking, dare-devil American by the name of Lem.* Nothing was too solemn for his witticism, and no position too dangerous or important for his caricature or hoax. Everything that came to his mind had a distorted and ludicrous appearance. His eyes were like those laboratorial lenses, which represent the bodies seen through them to be in every position but the right one. Even his dreams were of conundrums, quaint sayings, and funny anecdotes. Consequently such Chinamen as he met had to stand, or run, before his volley of comical shot. Although he was perpetually annoying

* Mr. Lemuel E. Harris, of Scodunk, N. Y.

them with some trick or caricature, they seldom became angry or showed any disposition to resent them, except by returning his jokes in the way they were sent.

One day when we were making a short trip inland from Shanghai, Lem placed a very small American flag in the apex of a chair Coolie's hat, unbeknown to the wearer, and kept joking him upon his "Melican (American) proclivities." The flag, being made of paper, was printed only upon one side, leaving the other side clean and white.

The Chinaman soon discovered it, and took it carefully down, without uttering a word to Lem, who was so hidden by the close cover of the sedan that he could not observe the Coolie's actions. When the spare Coolie came up to spell him, the possessor of the flag sat down beside the path, and with a piece of red clay drew upon the blank side of the flag a caricature of one of the Chinese devils. He then hastened on and caught up with us in time to take his turn at the chair. Before relieving the other, however, he cautiously inserted the flag-stick in the top of Lem's sedan, just over his head, and left it to flutter there with the American colors upon one side and a dancing devil upon the other. All this while Lem kept joking the Coolie, in a blind way, about the flag, supposing, as he had heard no demonstration, that the Coolie had not discovered it. To make the Chinaman's trick the more pointed, the inhabitants along the path seeing the flag at a little distance, and supposing that some Chinese official was passing, flocked to the chair, and wonderingly looked in to see the "Melican devil" supposed to answer to the description without, — and to laugh when they found it only a "long-whiskered barbarian." All of which was inexplicable to Lem until the presence of the gathering crowd caused the laughing Coolies to set down his chair and tear up the flag.

At another time Lem had secured two chair Coolies who could talk pigeon English, and he kept them chattering away just for the fun of it. But they soon discovered that he was making "game" of them, and answered only the most direct questions. All Chinamen who can speak pigeon English suppose it to be the real language of England, and these chair Coolies informed Lem that they were sure their language was right and that he "speakee no proper." Lem laughed at them and said that if he could not speak better English than they did he would "go and hang himself"; whereupon they refused to talk at all. Shortly after we came to a stagnant pool or ditch in a rice-patch, over which had been thrown a single log, or pole. This log was about fifteen feet long, and had not been shorn of knots, while the recent stripping of the bark made it slippery and unsafe. Twice the foremost Coolie started upon the pole, at Lem's request, and fearing lest he should fall into the stream and drop the chair, as well as cover himself with mud, he withdrew, and set down the chair in order to get another pole, which lay but a short distance away. Lem stormed and ridiculed them for their timidity, and declaring that "an elephant could walk *that* log," leaped out of his chair and started upon a run along the pole. His haste, big feet, and stiff limbs, combined with the oily state of the pole, were too much for his equilibrium, and when about half-way over down he went — *swash* — into the slime-covered pool. The Coolies came running up in affright, and one waded in to assist him while the other gathered tufts of grass with which to brush his saturated and mire-covered clothes. Lem was taken out safely, and was made as comfortable by brushing and washing as a man in his circumstances could be, when one of the Coolies who had been the proudest of his "English," stepping a little on one side, with his arms akimbo, blew out a long, deep breath, and quaintly remarked: "*Mayhow Melican muchee talkee, but he no muchee walkee.*"

NUMBER THREE.

SCENE AT A JOSS-HOUSE.

DID you ever pause for a moment in the porch of a fashionable church, in America, to watch the eddies of the incoming flood as it gurgles and bubbles in through the outer door-way, whirls for an instant in the hall, and then moves steadily on, down the long aisle, to divide and subdivide into the side-passages and pews? In it will be seen the foolish fop, the gaudy miss, the gold-bedecked spinster, and the proud old banker, pausing for a moment in the entrance to arrange their gorgeous apparel, preparatory to a triumphal march down the wide aisle to the distant pew. Girls and boys, men and women come pouring in, all dressed in their richest and gayest attire, as if they were going to a festival or ball, instead of attending the worship of a God who hates arrogance and pride, and who cannot be deceived into the acceptance of a black or tainted soul, however much it may be gilded. Here and there are thoughtful, reverential ones, who seek the house of God for instruction in the way of His commandments; and occasionally a mourner whose broken, aching heart will cease its painful throbbings only in the house of prayer. If you have ever thoughtfully scanned such a tide you cannot soon forget the lesson which it teaches. For the gay apparel, personal ornaments, intelligent faces, carpeted aisles, cushioned pews, philosophical sermons, and words of comfort, whether the proud incomers appreciate it or not, are monuments to the value of the Christian religion. Even the most silly devotee of fashion, who flaunts her jewels with shameful defiance in the sanctuary of the Most High God, is indebted to the religion whose house she desecrates for all those ornaments and comforts. The heathen do not possess them. In none but Christian lands do we find comfort and happiness, as an outgrowth of the religion; and how foolish it does seem for man to decorate himself in pride, and march into church, saying by his demeanor, "Look at me, and see what I have done," instead of saying, as a reasonable being should say: "Look at me, and see what *God has done.* The refining and enlightening influence of Christianity has taken us literally out of mental darkness, and given to us a thousand pleasures of which the heathen never knew. We eat, drink, walk, ride, sing, read, and sleep amid luxuries which the hea-

then could not appreciate if he possessed them. We erect beautiful works of art, and with the aid of God's natural laws adorn our dwellings, parks, and highways in a way that would astonish the dull senses of an unchristian people. All this beauty and pleasure, education and refinement is the legitimate result of that personal and mental freedom which the religion of Christ carries with it wherever it goes. Yet with all these facts before them men often enter the doors of the church conscious only of their own importance. They even venture to deny the divinity of Christ while wearing his livery, and venture to speak ill of him while disciplining their minds by the light which he has given. How different with the heathen! Although their faith cannot quiet the fears and pangs of the mourner, give instruction to the ignorant, nor refine the manners or thoughts of the tacit believer, yet they enter not into its courts with pride, or show ingratitude when they find themselves in comfortable circumstances.

Sitting by the gate of a Boodist temple one evening, I watched the devotees as they came and went, endeavoring to ascertain by their appearance what errands had brought them there. Although it was one of the finest temples which I had seen in China, yet it was a far different place from the well-proportioned and beautifully decorated churches of America. The entrance to the enclosure was through a ponderous gateway of timber, from the top of which two hideous wooden dragons frowned upon the visitors. The fence which, with the exception of the gate, entirely surrounded the temple was made of rough splinters, which were so decayed and broken that a boy could leap over at almost any point. Within the fence, and around the little hut or temple, the ground was strewn with rubbish, or rooted up by swine, and supported here and there a clumpy growth of weeds and low brambles. The temple was about twenty feet square, and was built of wood, with the exception of the roof, which was covered with long red tiles. It was about twelve feet high, and was ornamented, or rather disfigured, at the eaves and ridge with ill-carved dragons of a repulsive design. The entrance was through a narrow door in the side, which opened directly into the idol-chamber, where the image of Boodah was placed. This chamber was a large square room hung about with embroidered flags, paper images, soiled tinsel, and tassels, without regard for symmetry, while upon several richly carved tables was to be seen little images of wood, bronze, and stone, sitting, lying, or standing, as though they had been scattered promiscuously about by the armful. Several large metal vases stood about the room, some containing flowers, others joss-sticks and dried fruit. The idol, before which the

OUR WHEELBARROW RIDE.—Page 278.

long-robed priest chanted and bowed, sat cross-legged on a stand with his arms folded, his head erect, and his back against the wall. His long mustache streamed down to his shoulders, while his ruddy cheeks, black eyes, and embroidered cap gave him the appearance of a rollicking wine-bibber. Before him were burning bunches of little splinters in goblets or on platters, and a number of hanging-baskets of bamboo and beads, containing garlic, rice, and cake. The floor was unswept and filthy, while the dust from many feet arose in little clouds and begrimed the tapestry, wall, and idol in a most disgusting way. The night was dark and cloudy, but the gateway, enclosure, and temple were so illuminated with Chinese lanterns of gay design, that it presented a rather inviting aspect, when seen from the dark and uneven pathway. It was not a festal day, but the death of some noted man had recalled to their senses many careless ones, and the stream of worshippers was much larger that night than usual. Merchant, broker, farmer, and laborer came to renew their vows, and stopped at the gateway, *heathen-like*, to take off such unnecessary ornaments as they wore upon their persons, lest the idol should be offended at their pride. If their long cues had been rolled up during the day, they were now carefully taken down and stroked into respectable smoothness, so that the wearer might not appear in the idol-chamber in a plight that indicated disrespect or carelessness. One old man appeared in the gateway light in whose short frock there was a rent about the size of his hand. He was evidently in great haste, and made a pause in the gateway to regain his breath after a long and tedious walk. While standing there, his gray hair shining in the lantern light, and his limbs trembling with fatigue, he suddenly discovered the hole in his frock. His countenance fell in an instant, giving to his face an expression of disappointment such as children sometimes assume when a cherished toy falls to the floor and is shattered into fragments. He lifted his skirt and looked closely at the rent; drawing it together with his thumb and finger, as if endeavoring to ascertain how it would look when repaired. He then placed the palm of his hand over it and turned about to assure himself that no one would notice it if he kept his hand in that position. But the old look of disappointment returned when he found that his hand was too small. He then tried to tuck it under, and pin the fold with a wooden splinter, but the cloth was too thick. At this failure he seemed for a while to be entirely at a loss to decide what should be his next movement. He began at last to unbutton the frock, and, pausing for a moment to consider the propriety of appearing before the God without an outer garment, he buttoned it again. Then turning from side to side he viewed the fringed spot from all possible positions, and finally deciding, with a sad sigh, that he was unfit to appear in the presence of Boodah, he turned sorrowfully away and disappeared in the darkness.

Around the gateway, flitting in and out of the fitful light, were a number of beggars whose filthy and diseased appearance was a most blood-chilling sight. Crutches, slings, bandages, patches and poultices disfigured their appearance, and the reckless exposure of wounds and sores made it painful to look at them. Sometimes a well-dressed Chinaman would toss a cash into their midst as he passed in, and the mass of human misery writhed and tumbled about the spot, forgetful of pain in their contest for a coin worth the one fifth part of a cent. One old woman brought her invalid son upon her back, and leaving him at the portal, through which her sex are not permitted to pass, she stood gazing wistfully up the lantern-hung pathway, while her sickly boy tottered up to the temple and crowded in at its glaring door-way. Several young men stopped in the reflection without to settle their quarrels and debts before entering the sacred precincts, while some paused before the entrance to collect their thoughts and determine what should be their confession and what their request, and to adopt a method for making them. One man paused, pulled off his wide hat, looked vacantly at the lanterns, moved his lips, stamped with his feet, scratched his head, and had a perplexed air about his movements, as if he had some great request to make and was unable to decide upon the way in which it should be done. At last a happy thought comes to his relief, and throwing up his head he walks cheerfully into the gateway and joins in the shadowy procession that hurries toward the "sacred presence." Thus they come and go, appearing from the gloom to flit for an instant in the light and then disappearing in darkness; a fair symbol of the religion they profess, which teaches them that an entrance into the world is an escape from gloom, and an exodus from it but the beginning of darkness and terror. Hours pass, and the stream becomes smaller and smaller, until there are only a few straggling, poorly-dressed Coolies coming at long intervals; and then the nasal chant of the priest is discontinued, the great gong without ceases its roar, and the keeper puts out the lights in the temple and gateway, leaving the spot, like the faith to which it is dedicated, cheerless, chilly, damp and dark.

NUMBER FOUR.

CHINESE AMUSEMENTS.

IF the tones of the gongs which deafen your ears at each-dinner hour in your fashionable hotel suit your taste for music, then perhaps you might be able to appreciate a Chinese concert. But if that offends your ear, then be careful, while travelling in China, to go as far as possible from every concert-hall or temple. Such a noise! The roof seems to shake and the earth to tremble with the vibration, while the sensations of an auditor are like those of a person standing close beside the track when the engine of the lightning express thunders by. I attended one of the native concerts, and, while I hold to my present determination, I shall never go again. It was held in the hall of the theatre, and was given to celebrate some religious or national anniversary, the importance of which depended upon the prosperity of the nation during the previous year. There were two classes of musicians, — drummers and pipers; the former outnumbering the latter at least two to one. The whole company numbered about sixty, and marched around the stage without order or plan, and each thumped or piped with all his strength. The pipes were made of reeds, in the ends of which were inserted mouthpieces or whistles, while the drums were nothing more than pans, kettle-drums, and ordinary gongs, accompanied by "bones" and wooden cymbals. There seemed to be no more harmony or system to the vocal part of the performance than there was to the instrumental; for each man beat his gong, blew his whistle, clapped his cymbals, and yelled, without regard to tune or time, and paid so little heed to his steps, that many a head was thumped and many an elbow scarred before the performance closed.

They were all men, and were said to be "professional performers on the gong and pipe." But if they were "professional," it must be a strange performance indeed where amateurs are admitted to the stage! It was but a few moments that I could stay in the hall, so deafening and chilling was the din, and while I was there the only vocal sounds which I could detect above the roar and rattle was a prolonged and oft-repeated "Ya-a-a-e-e ya-a-a-e-e!" Our interpreter stated that the musicians were "hailing the spring," and that they would keep up that drumming and screaming for ten or twelve hours, with little or no variation.

It is a characteristic of the Chinese, that the more they listen to musical sounds the coarser and more boisterous must it become to suit their "growing tastes." Like those other antipodal customs which bid them wear white at funerals and black at marriage, print books from right to left, value the friendship of one who presents a coffin, and condemn a thing when they intend to praise — it cultivates coarseness instead of refinement.

More surprising does this seem to me, since I listened to the song of "Tramp, tramp," as rendered by some Chinese pupils of a missionary in Singapore. For these scholars showed beyond controversy an apt and discriminating ear for harmony and melody, and sang that well-known American song with all the parts, in the most pleasing and artistic manner. But the missionary declared that he had no hope of making musicians of his classes, — he had found that the more they practised the less appreciative they had become.

Chinese theatres, with all their age and celebrity, can scarcely be declared either amusing or instructive to the European or American spectator. The plot is usually very simple, being a journey or a marriage, or a fight without those complications which make the plays of Western lands so interesting and exciting. The actors perform upon a platform without curtain or scenery, and have an "operatic" way of drawling or screeching the vocal part and of wandering about the stage in violation of all the rules which govern actors elsewhere. The men, boys, girls, priests, gods, and demons which frequent the stage do not consider themselves of any importance to the play, and if they should happen to be ill, wish to smoke a pipe, or eat a meal, they will absent themselves without procuring substitutes, and the play seems to go on just as well without them. Everything is left to the spectator's imagination; and, as it will be more or less interesting as the auditor's imagination is fertile or barren, the success of a play in China depends more on the audience than on the actors. If a man is supposed to be in a ship, he carries a pole with a sail attached and beats a gong. If he wishes to act the part of a boatman, he carries a pair of oars under his arm. Sometimes the actors wear placards, i. e. when the audience is dull and unappreciative, — upon which are written, "This is the god of good luck." "This boy is a gardener," "This woman is the wife of the money-broker," "This player is a good fellow," "This actor is a bad man"; all of which assists the audience in "guessing out" the meaning of the play. It sometimes happens, that the spectators are mistaken about the intent of the players, and go on imagining a tragedy, when perhaps it is a comedy, or think that there is a thrilling love romance when it is all about thieves and money-brokers. The actors play from early morning until far into the night, and visitors come in and stay an hour or more, and having *imagined* an act go to their business until evening, when they come again and imagine another act. It sometimes happens that a company more venturesome and gifted than their class, play the parts with more fidelity to nature, and make their meaning too apparent to be mistaken; but such plays are seldom popular, and cannot, like the others, be played for weeks without any decrease of interest. Several attempts have been made to introduce scenery and more appropriate costumes, but like all innovations upon established custom, they met with a cold reception.

The Chinese love games of chance, and are said to be acquainted with over one hundred different methods of gambling. Old and young, male and female, play these games, believing that the result is the decree of the gods or spirits, who control everything that is left to chance. Gambling may be said to be the "national game" of China. For all the spare hours given to recreation are spent in playing games with forfeits; and in nothing do they seem to take so much pride as in the possession of winnings. The usual mode of gaming now popular in the lower provinces is that of betting on the number of coin contained in a handful of *cash*. The betting is done by a number of Chinamen, while a disinterested party is selected to take out as many coins as his hand will hold from a large pile, and to count them out by "twos," "fours," or "sevens." Sometimes parties bet that the handful will have a certain number of "fours," and others accept the wager, winning or losing on the count. At the regular gambling halls, the bet is usually made upon the number that will remain after counting out all the "fours" in the pile. This is done by taking a handful of coin at random from a pile, and placing it on a table, after which a disinterested party counts out the coin, four at a time. The number of coin which are left after the last "four" has been taken will determine the bet. If there are three, or two, or one, or it comes out "even," the person staking his money on the lucky number gets the whole of the amount wagered upon the other numbers. If a Coolie states that he wagers ten cents upon number "three," and, after all the "fours" are taken away, there be three coins left, he will get forty cents, while if there are none, or one, or two left, he looses his stake, and it goes to the party who bet on the winning number.

Bets are often made on the direction from which the wind will blow on the morrow, on the side that will come up, when a coin is thrown in the air and allowed to fall upon the ground, on the number of grains in a quart of barley, on the sex of an unborn child, on the year that a person will die, on quoits, marbles, dice, dominos, and on a thousand things which may be the subject of speculation or risk.

Kite-flying is a favorite amusement with old men, and ball-playing with children. Dolls, toys, and pictures are manufactured in large numbers, but are sought more by old people than by the children. Jugglery and legerdemain are the most exciting amusements aside from gambling, and a successful performer will never want for an audience in China. The favorite feat is that of keeping eight wooden balls flying in the air, with the hands, head, and feet; and so directing their motions as to represent fountains, balls, wheels, stars, &c. The skill and agility displayed in that feat does seem to be almost miraculous; yet the juggler seldom acts as though it was a great task, but will keep the balls flying for hours if the auditors happen to desire it.

Another popular amusement is found in the making and guessing of riddles. At some seasons, and especially "New Year's," the mandarins and scholars have lanterns hung at their door, on which are printed several of these riddles, and a notice is given that whoever succeeds in guessing either one will receive a certain reward or present. But the making of riddles is not confined to any class or time. Even the Coolies on board ship devote their attention to them. Here are two which occupied the crowd a considerable time before they were able to answer.

"When is it that the faster a man walks the less progress he makes on his journey?"

"*Ans.* When he walks from stem to stern on a moving steamer."

"What is it that moves itself, without having life or assistance, is flat and round, and will easily carry a load which ten thousand million of Chinamen could not lift?"

"*Ans.* The ocean."

A Chinese money-broker in Yokohama, Japan, propounded the following to a number of emigrants bound to California, who went on shore at that port while the vessel was taking in cargo and coal.

"What kind of men sell a home to own it, leave their families in order to live with them, go among enemies to find friends, spend their money in order to get it, and become prisoners to be free?"

With astonishing unanimity the crowd of Coolies replied, "*The Emigrants to America.*"

NUMBER FIVE.

OUR WHEELBARROW RIDE.

WE were homeward bound. That is to say, we were going to Cheefoo; from which place, several days before, we started for the Tomb of Confucius. A curious quartette we made — the driver, interpreter, Lem and I — while lumbering along over hills and ravines in one of the most awkward carts upon which my eyesight ever fell. Our friends at Cheefoo had told us that we would have trouble on the route, either at the Gold Mines or at our destination; but little did we care. The greater the hardships the more meritorious the pilgrimage. Lem said that we were going "to the tomb of some old fellow who lived several years ago, but of whom nobody but antiquarians and newspaper reporters had ever heard," and he wanted something exciting to quiet his conscience and furnish a reasonable excuse for such a foolhardy trip. However, we accomplished the journey, after passing many sleepless nights on filthy mats and eating many half-cooked meals.

We had been watched by government spies and made to pay tribute to the Yen-chow-foo descendants of ancient Philosophers. We had been told how Confucius and Mencius had trod the paths in which we were walking. How, according to the most celebrated Chinese book, called *Shoo King,* there was once a great flood there, and that later there were great battles on the plains we were crossing. We had seen the labyrinth-like temple of Confucius at Keo-fu-han, with its tablets, carved dragons, images of that philosopher and his disciples, vases of marble and bronze over three thousand years old; and its gardens of cypress, with their massive gates and rustic bridges. We had entered the enclosures and looked upon that mound, said to be the tomb of the great philosopher and moralist, and which is covered with a growth of trees and partially hid by a huge slab with Confucius's name and deeds engraven upon it. We had wandered over the "sacred mountains," looked at the graves of old kings and great scholars, saw where the disciples of Confucius sat and debated, and where they were buried; and we drew inspiration from the romantic shades where the greatest poets of China "loved and sung," and where that great and good man, *Yu,* is said to have worked such wonders. Our guide had rattled away at jaw-breaking Chinese names and classical quotations, until we were almost ready to order him to hold his tongue; and we had been stared at and mocked by the natives until we wished ourselves "well out of old *Chow's* territory."

We had taken a somewhat circuitous course on our return to look upon that "wandering river," which floods the country and finds a new bed and a new mouth nearly every year.* Natives had teased us for presents, boatmen had quarrelled over our passage at the ferries, and hotel-keepers had vied with each other in furnishing us suitable entertainment. But nevertheless we had met with no serious obstacle, and had seen scarcely enough of adventure to relieve the dull monotony of such a long cart-journey. But just as we were winding along the side of a steep hill, a short distance from a town called Whang-han, the axletree of the cart gave way, and Lem, myself, and the baggage went headlong after the mule, which the accident sent rolling down a stony declivity. The driver and the interpreter, who were walking beside the cart at the time, at once made a rush for the mule, and managed to push him into a standing position, while Lem gave vent to his rage in rather emphatic language, and assisted me to pull my bruised limbs from under the pieces of lumber, bundles of straw and provisions which came after us from the overturned cart. What a fix! Nearly one hundred and fifty miles from the seaport, in a country

* Yellow River.

infested with banditti, without a cart, with an angry driver and a dissatisfied interpreter. What was to be done? At first we had hoped to be able to repair the cart and proceed as before, but it was so broken by the fall, that, without a suitable piece of lumber for an axletree, and the tools with which to shape it, we could do nothing.

For a long time we stood about the wreck, discussing various expedients, and rejecting each as it was made; and it was not until the decline of the sun warned us to adopt something at once, that we concluded to leave the cart, driver, and mule, and proceed on foot. We were to stop at a tea-house, the location of which seemed well known to the driver and interpreter, and wait there until the former had time to get assistance, repair the damage, and bring up the team. We had not proceeded far, however, picking our way along the side of the hills, before Lem began to tire of carrying his large, crowded carpet-bag, and declared that he *could not* walk "seven *Li* farther," which our guide said was the distance to the tea-house where we must stop. At least he "*would rest*," and suiting the action to the word, sat down upon his carpet-bag, and, as he himself has since declared, "sighed for Scodunk, New York."

He was just about to respond to our urgent solicitation to proceed, when his attention was called to the little butterfly-looking wheelbarrow sails which seemed to be skimming along the valley below us. We had often noticed them before, but never had seen as many, or looked upon a landscape of cottage, village, rice-fields, and stream to which they seemed to add such a charm. Shimmering into the trees or behind the houses and out again, flitting from block to block of the drain-cut plantations, and fluttering strangely in the sun when the owners let go the sail to "tack" or make a stop. "Why not hire a wheelbarrow?" was Lem's first question after we had gazed for a few moments upon the varied landscape and watched the zigzag progress of those "land sail-boats." "Why not?" echoed I, looking at our interpreter for an answer. But he objected, saying that they were dangerous vehicles.

"Why dangerous?"

"Because they would tip over."

Lem scoffed at the idea of tipping over, and sat down again determined to wait until "doom's day," if the interpreter did not see fit to go down and hire one of "them air things." It was more than a mile to the village, and I objected, telling Lem that we were in danger of losing our guide or of being attacked in his absence; but he was immovable, and I resigned myself to the fates, and waited through an anxious hour for the appearance of the interpreter with a wheelbarrow. At last we saw him coming, slowly winding up the hillside accompanied by a Coolie with a wheelbarrow *without a sail.* Lem was quite displeased at the idea of a wheelbarrow-ride without the assistance of the wind, and swore that he would not ride in it, and that Arr Choo should go back for another. On the arrival of the clumsy conveyance, however, we found that the sail had been taken down because it would be of no assistance in coming up the hill. But the driver thought that it might avail us in driving the wheelbarrow down the declivities, when we were once fairly started. I thought so too, and objected to its being set; but Lem wanted it, "just for romance," and the fluttering, ragged sheet was unfurled. The wheelbarrow had but one wheel, and that was so inserted that a half of it was below and the other half above the floor or bottom of the barrow.* But the felly was so wide that it was not a difficult matter to keep the barrow upright, under ordinary circumstances. We had seen conveyances of this kind several times before, since leaving Cheefoo, but never after this pattern, and we found that the protruding portion of the wheel, on the inside, was going to be a great inconvenience. But the more awkward the machine the better suited was Lem, and he bounced into the barrow at the motion of the owner as though he was very impatient for a ride.

* See illustration.

"Say! you there," said he after seating himself on the side and trying to pull up one corner of the flapping sail. "I say! you; cap'n of this ere craft, can't yer take a reef in this ere machine?"

The Chinaman, who doubtless had never seen a European before, nodded and scraped and smiled as if he would have us believe that he understood every word. Arr Choo repeated the question in Chinese, and received the reply that the sail was too little even now, and that it "no go fast." After a little persuasion I got into the barrow and sat upon the side-board opposite Lem; for there was scarcely room inside for our feet and Lem's carpet-bag, which, however, with some difficulty we managed to cram into the corners away from the dirt-throwing wheel. "All right; go it!" shouted Lem; and after the order had been repeated by Arr Choo, the Coolie seized the lower corners of the sail and quickly tying them to the cross-piece, ran to the long handles and lifted them from the ground. Just then Lem shifted his position, a little puff of wind filled the sail, and in an instant over went the wheelbarrow, while we, ill-fated passengers, landed, as Lem afterwards declared, "with our heads whar our feet 'd orter been." The carpet-bag went in one direction, Lem's hat in another, and the wheelbarrow with the Coolie in another, and everything but Lem and I was very much scattered. We fell together, and so mixed were our extremities that Lem groaned out, "O my knee!" and afterwards made up his mind that it was me who was hurt. After some persuasion and more cursing on the part of Lem, and a little sly laughing on the part of Arr Choo, we entered the wheelbarrow again. Lem in the mean time nursing his patience by singing the song of Mother Goose, which says that

> "The wheelbarrow broke, his wife had a fall;
> And down came wheelbarrow, wife and all."

This time fortune and the wind favored us, and away we went under the skilful guidance of the Coolie, winding along the narrow path, now descending, now ascending; here near the edge of a precipice, there through a narrow cut, until the ride, which at first filled us with fear, became pleasing and comfortable. The sail being fastened only at the top and bottom, and even there to hoops that would turn upon the mast, it always kept its broadside to the wind, no matter in what direction the vehicle was turned. The skill was displayed in keeping the barrow upright in the gusts, and so turning in the selection of the path as to keep the wind behind the sail.

Once he was obliged to take several "tacks" before he could reach the top of a knoll, and he did it by turning the wheelbarrow so as to receive the wind fairly in the sail, and, after a great *momentum* had been gained, wheeling suddenly about and pushing it as far as possible against the wind. It was a most exhilarating ride: along the mountain-side, overlooking a beautiful valley, and fanned by the little air eddies made in the sail. For more than an hour we rode on our way, sometimes as fast as the Coolie could run, and at other times very slow, and were beginning to think of seeing the residence for which we were in search, when we came out upon the brow of a mountain from which another one of the most varied and pleasing landscapes of the world was presented to our view. Here the mountain-side was an easy slope while the path which led down to the valley was nearly straight, and appeared from our station to be even and smooth. When we learned that we must descend to the valley, Lem caught hold of the side of the barrow, as if to brace himself, and shouted, "Give him ther reins, mister? Mind yer bearins and let 'er rip."

I protested. But as everything must be translated, the Coolie, who understood Lem's gestures, had started before my commands reached him, and it was too late then to stop. I would have leaped out, but I was afraid that such action would upset my companion, so I held on the best I could and determined to abide the consequences. The wind was "a little abaft the beam," as the sailors say, and for the first few yards pressed heavily against the sail, starting us off at race-horse speed. We had not proceeded far before the wheelbarrow outstripped the wind, and the sail flapped back with a terrific bang against the mast and we were nearly thrown from the wheelbarrow by the sudden check put upon our speed. With another gust the sail again filled and on we sped as before. Soon the path became stony and crooked, so that the Coolie in his efforts to balance the vehicle turned first one side down and then the other; lifted the handles as high as his shoulders and again let them down so low that they dragged upon the ground, tipping us about in a way that required our entire strength to hold on. The path grew steeper and rougher, the wind grew fresher, Lem's hold upon the side-board more insecure, and the retroaction of the sail became more frequent and forcible, until the ride was nothing but a series of neck-breaking jerks and dizzy oscillations. Bumping over the stones, or throwing up clouds of dirt, the wheel buzzed between our feet like a circular saw, while the Coolie with a nimbleness and a display of strength which would do a star circus performer credit, threw himself into all manner of attitudes, and still guided the barrow, although it would have required the entire attention of any ordinary man to have kept his feet in the path when proceeding at such speed, without being burdened with the care of such an uncertain vehicle. At last the path became too crooked, even for the skilled Coolie, and on being pressed with a strong gust of wind at a sudden turn in the track, he struck across the dry field, thinking to enter the path again at the next curve. But Lem, who was getting nearly exhausted, and who considered a departure from the path to be a dangerous and foolish experiment, suddenly called out in angry tones, "Look o' here, whar are you going to, you old fool?" The Coolie could not understand the words, but the anger which he saw in Lem's face seemed to disconcert him, and while trying to hold back upon the handles, the barrow gave a sudden lurch, and in attempting to prevent an overturn in one direction he put forth too much strength, and with a sudden swoop, just as Lem screamed, "Thunderation! Hold on!" over came the wheelbarrow and its contents, with myself at the bottom.

Lem scratched his shins and groaned, forgetful of his carpet-bag, half filled with sand, and his tall hat crushed in the wheel, while I, until the arrival of Arr Choo, limped about, looking for a pool of water with which to wash the sand from my eyes and mouth. This fully satisfied us with land-sailing, and ever after, when our carts failed us, Lem and I demurely went on foot.

Cambridge: Printed by Welch, Bigelow, and Company.

www.ingramcontent.com/pod-product-compliance
Lightning Source LLC
LaVergne TN
LVHW010212110826
845151LV00004B/1064

* 9 7 8 1 4 2 5 5 2 8 4 2 3 *